Does God Feel Your Pain?

H. Wayne House
& William Grover

HARVEST HOUSE PUBLISHERS

EUGENE, OREGON

Cover by Garborg Design Works, Savage, Minnesota

DOES GOD FEEL YOUR PAIN?
Copyright © 2009 by H. Wayne House and William Grover
Published by Harvest House Publishers
Eugene, Oregon 97402
www.harvesthousepublishers.com

Library of Congress Cataloging-in-Publication Data
    House, H. Wayne.
    Does God feel your pain? / H. Wayne House and William Grover
        p. cm.
    ISBN 978-0-7369-2476-4 (pbk.)
    1. Suffering—Religious aspects—Christianity. 2. Pain—Religious aspects—Christianity. I. Grover, William, 1940- II. Title.
    BT732.7.H68 2009
    231'.8—dc22
                                                                                            2008039898

Printed in the United States of America

09 10 11 12 13 14 15 16 17 / BP-NI / 10 9 8 7 6 5 4 3 2 1

To Virginia Ellen Chatham
—Wayne

To my good wife, Jan
—Bill

Acknowledgments

We wish to thank those who have been involved in various aspects of this book. An author is unable to move from the first words of his book to its completion without a number of people contributing necessary components to its successful production. First, we must give thanks to our wives for their encouragement and patience. Writing a book takes away time from our loved ones who nonetheless have supported us throughout this endeavor. Also, much appreciation must be expressed to Robert Drouhard for his excellent research on our behalf, checking items and endnotes. His work helped to ensure a much more accurate and better book. We also wish to thank the editor, Steve Miller, for his careful attention to detail in the course of working on the book and moving it toward its publication.

—H. Wayne House and William Grover

Dec 21, 2012 Fr.
Fron Cindy Kelly

Contents

Foreword

I live with chronic pain.

Pain distracts, distorts, and depresses me. It screams for attention and there is little relief. It keeps me from doing things I always took for granted. I used to play racquetball, exercise with a personal trainer, work in my yard for hours, and detail my cars. I love working with my hands, sweating, and all this has been my "diversion therapy" from the stress and strain of life. But pain has robbed me of these activities.

In 2001 I started having hip pain. It took several trips to the doctors, tests, and referrals to discover a host of spine issues. Sometimes called "degenerative disc disease," I've gone the gambit looking for cures and relief. I have had two back surgeries. I've seen chiropractors. I've had acupuncture. I've been to different kinds of physical therapists. I've been to pain management specialists *many* times. I've gotten multiple "second" opinions. I've had MRIs, scans, nerve conduction tests, myelograms, and other tests beyond memory. I've seen extraordinary physicians at Loyola, Northwestern. I've been to the Mecca of Medicine: Mayo Clinic. I've even drunk some expensive juice that's supposed to cure all my ailments and make my skin softer. And to this day, well-meaning people send me cures in the mail. I'm still in agony.

Pain has also affected my life, my job, and my relationships. A person who lives with high pain levels is not pleasant. When you hurt so much you cannot sleep, read, sit, stand, or walk without pain screaming at you, you are not much fun to be around. I can be short with my kids, bristle at people's petty issues, and withdrawn from social contacts. My co-workers took the brunt of this sometimes and unfortunately, questioned my judgment.

At some point—and I cannot tell anyone when—you change your pace on all of this. The magnificent obsession of finding relief starts to fade. You begin to decide, *I'm going to have to find some way to live with chronic pain and not be a horrible person.*

It's like pushing a wet string uphill.

The jury is still out on my life of pain. I don't have any answers. I can tell you, I do not ask the Lord, "Why?" but I do ask Him, "How?" "How am I supposed to live this way? How am I to serve you like this? How can I be the kind of husband and father and friend I used to be?"

At times, I am desperate. I cry. I pray. Many times, when the pain is so intense and I am flat on the floor, I beg Him, "Would you please help me?"

My wife, Cindy, has been remarkable. She never complains. She never gets angry at me. I know most marriages do not do well when one spouse takes ill. For this, I truly bless God. I also have better friends than Job. I have friends who have been through horrible illnesses, major surgeries, organ transplants, and who live with MS and pain levels that make mine look like child's pain. Jim, Dave, Robert, and Barbara understand. And they are patient and loving and encouraging, unlike many well-intentioned Christians. They put up with a lot of my junk and still love me. Even when I have not talked to them in a while, I know they are faithful and silent witnesses to me.

They are a towering blessing.

I do not consider myself successful in living with pain. I consider myself a lousy patient. But what I have learned is this:

1. Pain is relative but real.
2. My life has changed. I don't like it, but I'm learning to live with it.
3. I hate being defined by pain.
4. I hate being asked about my pain all the time.

5. I must choose to find joy.

6. I must look for blessings.

7. Christ loves me and knows all about my pain.

8. I want 2 Corinthians 1:3-7 to be a reality in my life.

Join Drs. House and Grover as they navigate us through this journey. We have one Great Physician and it is to Him all of us—sin-sick sinners—must come.

2 Corinthians 1:3-7

Dr. Michael Easley
President Emeritus
Moody Bible Institute

Preface

Pain is one of the experiences of life that all of us share in common, whether the pain is physical, emotional, mental, or spiritual. All of us know what it means for everything to fall around us, when we find ourselves looking outside of ourselves for an answer to the suffering in our own lives and the misery that we observe in the larger world in which we live. Where is God in all of this?

Those who reject the God presented in the Bible either disbelieve in God altogether or create a god who is powerless to change the world or does not really care about our difficulties. It is common in our post-Christian West to express sarcasm and skepticism about Christian faith in God, who has promised never to leave nor forsake us.

Those of us, however, who have embraced the God of Abraham, Isaac, and Jacob, and received the Lord Jesus into our lives as Savior, have a different attitude toward personal pain and global struggles. We do not deny natural and moral evil, but believe that there is a reason for these evils in the world that are distinguished from the good acts of God at the beginning of earth's creation and the culmination of His plans to bring an end and resolution to sin, sickness, and catastrophe.

In this book, we seek to put pain in perspective so that we can see how it fits into the overall plan of God for His world and demonstrate that it is not incongruent with His love or power. First, we need to understand the reality and nature of pain, and how suffering in this life, though not created by God, is actually used by God to glorify Him and benefit us. Second, we need to come to understand the God of biblical revelation. In so doing, we will not seek to bring Him down to the level of finite humanity to make us feel better. Rather, we will worship Him as the exalted God that He is, and marvel at how the sovereign, transcendent Creator of the universe has humbled Himself to reach into our lives to bring comfort and assistance to us, ultimately in the coming of Jesus the Messiah. The willingness of God to suffer in the humanity of Jesus welds together God's concern with God's understanding of our distress.

And finally, we need to come to understand how we may embrace the human lot brought on by the fall of mankind. We don't do this to avoid the human predicament, nor deny it as is true in Eastern religion, but to be willing to share in the sufferings of Christ, to be able to understand the pain of others around us, and in the end, to be victorious through pain in anticipation of the final day, when we will experience pain no longer.

Part One:

The Reality of Human Pain and How God Relates to It

Chapter One

God and Human Suffering

D o you sometimes feel as though God doesn't care? It is difficult to express such sentiments aloud, but in your mind, in times of quiet, do such thoughts invade your inner sanctum? He is so far beyond us that we might wonder if He is really near, particularly when we have had to face a major crisis, or the loss of a loved one. This doubt might be even more real when we gain a greater appreciation for God's glory, majesty, and greatness. How can a being such as God care for someone as small as me?

These kinds of feelings and hidden doubts are common to each of us because of the difficulties of life that come our way. The man Eliphaz, one of Job's "comforters," acknowledged this common experience when he said, "Yet man is born to trouble, as the sparks fly upward" (Job 5:7). There can be no denial, except by those who believe life is just an illusion, that we humans are frail in body and spirit. The level of physical, emotional, and spiritual struggles may vary from individual to individual, but all of us know the pain of the death of loved ones, emotional highs and lows as we encounter the unexpected changes in life's fortunes, and the physical pains that come from accidents, assaults from others, and just growing older. Often, like Job, when his body ached in agony, we cry out for an answer:

Why is light given to him who is in misery, and life to the
bitter of soul, who long for death, but it does not come,
and search for it more than hidden treasures; who rejoice
exceedingly, and are glad when they can find the grave?
Why is light given to a man whose way is hidden, and
whom God has hedged in? For my sighing comes before I
eat, and my groanings pour out like water. For the thing I
greatly feared has come upon me, and what I dreaded has
happened to me. I am not at ease, nor am I quiet; I have
no rest, for trouble comes (Job 3:20-26).

One of my former students with whom I (Wayne) have developed
a close relationship was in wonderful health until six years ago. He was
energetic, vibrant, each year running marathons for various causes.
He had entered a doctoral program at a major university and married
a wonderful young woman. (I had the privilege of performing the
ceremony.) Everything looked bright for the future.

Then he went on a medical missions trip to Vietnam with his wife.
He was careful about what he ate in Vietnam, yet developed an illness
that incapacitated him. He thought it might be cancer or some other
disease, but eventually was diagnosed with an autoimmune disorder
from a bacteria received, most likely, from using the local water for
brushing his teeth while in Vietnam. His strength was taken away
and he was in constant pain. Only now, after several years of affliction, has he gradually been able to resume his studies, travel a little,
and hold a job.

This raises some tough questions: How could God allow this to
happen, especially when this man went to Vietnam to serve God? Why
should he have to suffer so much when he had done nothing to call
for such difficulties in life? He and his wife had gone to Vietnam to
minister to others. Why should this calamity fall upon him?

From our perspective, it would make more sense for this to happen
to someone who did great evil. Why should this happen to one of
God's children?

Jesus, however, indicated that calamity may come upon anyone—

even those who do not appear to be terrible sinners (Luke 13:1-5). Furthermore, the fact that God does not bring immediate judgment on all humans because of their sins vividly demonstrates the extent of His great love and mercy.

The Bible provides examples of people who may help us understand how to deal with the incongruities and inequities of life. Men such as Abel, Job, David, Epaphroditus, Jesus, and Paul knew great difficulties, and we will look more closely at them and others in later chapters as we try to answer the question, Does God feel our pain?

The Reason for Human Suffering— Natural and Moral Evil

It is important for us to recognize that the human plight of suffering was not a necessary part of human experience until the entrance of sin into the world. As a result of Adam's fall (Romans 5:12-14) and the subsequent judgment of God (Genesis 3:15-19), the ramifications of sin are with each of us. Thus suffering is a result of sin, whether it comes from moral evil in the hearts and actions of other humans or from natural disasters that bring much misery on humanity. Neither source of suffering would have befallen man were it not for human rebellion against God.

Moral Evil

Before Adam's fall into sin, God pronounced everything in His creation as "very good" (Genesis 1:31). Since the fall, not only have people suffered, but creation itself is suffering due to man's sin and awaits renewal with the final redemption of the children of God (Romans 8:18-23).

Denial of this reality does not make suffering go away, but it does remove the only path to proper healing and redemption that God offers. One major component of Buddhist thought, and some pseudo-Christian religions, is the denial of suffering. The Buddha (thought to have been born Siddhartha Gautama, sometime around 560 B.C.) thought that it was possible to eliminate suffering by following certain practices. The Buddha became "enlightened" to the true state of the world and discovered what have become the Four Noble Truths central to Buddhism: all life is suffering, all suffering is caused by human desire, human suffering can be ended by ending human desire, and human desire can be ended by following the Eightfold Noble Path. This path is comprised of right understanding, right thought, right speech, right action, right livelihood, right effort, right mindfulness, and right concentration. One must understand that Buddhism sees an interconnectedness of all things and that the visual world is ultimately impermanent, or transitory. It is the attachment to this transitory world that causes suffering. If someone is in physical pain, it is because he is too attached to his transitory, physical body. If someone is suffering spiritually, it is because he has failed to realize the Noble Truths. Suffering becomes an exclusively internal problem one must overcome through adherence to Buddha's teachings.

Inherent in this religious thought is the denial of human depravity and the benefits of entering the sufferings of others to develop character. Often an attitude of unconcern for the needs and pains of other people is found within Eastern culture due the belief that sin and all reality is merely illusionary, or that each person should pay for bad karma. By contrast, in Christian thought, even though we recognize that we are sinners born into a sin-ridden world, there is nonetheless the need to minister to the needs and sufferings of others. One finds in the Bible a total rejection of the Eastern perspective. We may categorically say that all human pain and suffering is due to sin, but not all suffering comes to us because of personal sins that we have committed. Thus *some* suffering is caused by our desires, but desire certainly does not cause *all* suffering. Our difficulties may result from another person's evil acts. Even Jesus, who knew no sin, suffered (more on this in chapter 8).

There are some heretical religious groups that claim to be within the broad spectrum of Christianity that have denied the existence of sin and pain. These groups teach that reality is only mental or spiritual, and that pain and suffering are illusions that we must deny. If we do deny them, supposedly they will go away. This false notion has brought untold suffering upon children who have been denied appropriate medical care. Our purpose here is not to discuss groups such as Christian Scientists or other Mind Science religions,[1] but simply to point out that denial of sin and its fruits does *not* resolve our suffering. Rather, it contributes toward greater suffering and rejection of God's manner of healing us through the work of our deliverer, Jesus.

Natural Evil

Early Sunday morning, December 26, 2004, an earthquake measuring 9.0 on the Richter scale struck off the coast of Sumatra, Indonesia, and was followed by numerous strong aftershocks. It was the fourth-strongest earthquake in recorded history, and it resulted in powerful tsunamis (tidal waves)—some reaching almost 33 feet in height and traveling up to 40 miles an hour when they hit the shorelines of many land masses bordering the Indian Ocean. Large numbers of people were totally unprepared for such a disaster and had no advance warning. Entire villages disappeared under the massive walls of water. The combined death toll from the earthquake and subsequent tsunamis was over 227,000 people, and the material destruction is nearly incalculable.

Certainly this natural disaster, though massive, is but one of the thousands of disasters that occur every day of every year. A quick reading of the news reveals that humans suffer tremendously because of natural disasters. Pictures and videos of torrential floods, avalanches, mudslides, tornadoes, hurricanes, erupting volcanoes, and many other catastrophes daily fill news reports. Humans suffer in almost unimaginable ways due to calamities in the natural world. This suffering is real—it's not a result of the victims' failure to detach from the world or some kind of illusion.

As mentioned, the Bible says that on account of sin, creation itself suffers along with humanity. In Romans 8:21-22, the apostle Paul describes how nature is in "the bondage of corruption" and "groans and labors with birth pangs." The disasters we experience now are a result of the curse of sin. In Genesis 3:17 God told Adam, "Because you have heeded the voice of your wife, and have eaten from the tree of which I commanded you saying, 'You shall not eat of it': Cursed is the ground for your sake." This curse is to last until God recreates the heavens and earth at the end of time (Isaiah 65:17; Revelation 21:1). While God may cause calamity (Isaiah 45:7), we should not blame God for natural disasters because they are the result of sin and were not original to God's perfect creation.

The Necessity of a Proper Response to God

That pain is a part of human experience is a truism needing no debate since everyone has experienced pain, suffering, and difficulties to varying degrees. It is the *cause* of pain that is the point of contention, as well as how we deal with it. That is why we will first concern ourselves with the matter of how to respond to God in our pain. We will save the question of God's part in causing pain for a later chapter.

How should we respond to others, and even to God, in our times of distress? Job had multiple calamities befall him. The biblical story says that destruction came upon his property, his servants, and even his children. Some of the affliction came from the acts of evildoers, and some from natural disaster:

> Now there was a day when his sons and daughters were eating and drinking wine in their oldest brother's house; and a messenger came to Job and said, "The oxen were plowing and the donkeys feeding beside them, when the Sabeans raided them and took them away—indeed they have killed the servants with the edge of the sword; and I alone have escaped to tell you!"
>
> While he was still speaking, another also came and said, "The fire of God fell from heaven and burned up the sheep and the servants, and consumed them; and I alone have escaped to tell you!"
>
> While he was still speaking, another also came and said, "The Chaldeans formed three bands, raided the

camels and took them away, yes, and killed the servants with the edge of the sword; and I alone have escaped to tell you!"

While he was still speaking, another also came and said, "Your sons and daughters were eating and drinking wine in their oldest brother's house, and suddenly a great wind came from across the wilderness and struck the four corners of the house, and it fell on the young people, and they are dead; and I alone have escaped to tell you!" (Job 1:13-19).

At first Job seemed to be able to handle these tragedies in a manner far better than many of us might have. Listen to his words of trust in the goodness and greatness of God: "Naked I came from my mother's womb, and naked shall I return there. The LORD gave, and the LORD has taken away; blessed be the name of the LORD" (Job 1:21).

Instead of bitter railing against God, Job bowed down to worship the One who is in control of the world and all of life. What a testimony! In all of his pain, Job did not charge God with wrong (Job 1:22).

What is important in the midst of the suffering is how we respond to it. From time to time we hear of a famine in Africa, or of someone dear to us who has been diagnosed with an incurable disease. We feel a brief tug at our heart and may even say a prayer. But what if a major crisis were to happen to you? Or your child or spouse? How would you respond?

You have likely seen the many different ways people respond to the hard situations that life throws them. Some people seem to focus only on themselves and their misery, while others continue to focus on others, often saying little about their own problems. Some people thank God for the wonderful things He has done in their life and believe that they will grow through their suffering, while other people blame those around them, and particularly God, for their pain. How did you respond when your faith was tested?

How should we answer God in such times? The response from Job's wife is not one I would recommend: "Do you still hold fast to your integrity? Curse God and die!" (Job 2:9). Note how Job responded in unwavering faith: "Shall we indeed accept good from God, and shall we not accept adversity?" (Job 2:10).

A colleague and friend of mine (Wayne) for many years was an avid bike rider. He rode his bike for hundreds of miles at times. When he traveled nationally and internationally, he would take his bike on the plane so that he could continue his fitness program. A few years ago, however, in a freak accident, he lost control of his bike and sustained a head injury. Since then he has had terrible headaches that will not go away. He has found out that the only way to lessen the throbbing pain is to have massages. He tells me that this reduces about 80 percent of the pain. So that he could continue receiving massages, he became a massage therapist so he could trade off with fellow workers. What is his response to all of this? He says that God placed this problem in his life so he could have the opportunity to witness to people with whom he would have had no contact prior to his accident. This is making lemonade out of lemons, as is sometimes said. We can become sour toward others and God, or we can turn life's challenges into opportunities for thanksgiving.

Certainly, some people do not respond to adversity so well. Rather, they become bitter against God. I (Wayne) was recently talking with a friend, Larry, who is an African-American pastor who has had numerous encounters with people in times of need. One of the things that makes a pastor's job difficult is that he must "live" with his people through their crises—which may include sickness, the loss of a loved one, divorce, drug problems, or moral failures.

When I told Larry I was writing about how God is involved in caring for us in our pain, he told me, with considerable fervor, to discuss *why* some people get angry with God over the pangs of life—something he encounters often. This pastor knows what he is talking about. A lot of people are very angry with God. Some give no consideration to God in how they live. They rarely pray, if at all. They fail to embrace Him as Savior, or if they are Christians, as their Lord. They don't read the Bible to discover how to grow into a better knowledge of God's nature and His will. They don't take advantage of the empathetic work of the church. People like this can't seem to be consoled; they are simply angry at God for their problems and they shake their fists at Him.

To these people, there may be no answer because they might not truly be looking for one. Finding comfort from the God who loves and cares for His children requires an attitude of faith—not only the faith of a conqueror when everything is going well, but also the faith that perseveres in tough times (see Hebrews 11:35-40). The attitude described in the Beatitudes is necessary for those who want to find peace in times of trouble:

> Blessed are the poor in spirit, for theirs is the kingdom of heaven.
> Blessed are those who mourn, for they shall be comforted.
> Blessed are the meek, for they shall inherit the earth.
> Blessed are those who hunger and thirst for righteousness, for they shall be filled.
> Blessed are the merciful, for they shall obtain mercy.
> Blessed are the pure in heart, for they shall see God.
> Blessed are the peacemakers, for they shall be called sons of God.
> Blessed are those who are persecuted for righteousness' sake, for theirs is the kingdom of heaven (Matthew 5:3-10).

Those who find comfort, fulfillment, mercy, the presence of God, and peace are those who recognize their inadequacies and who are proactive in doing what is right before God. As the old hymn says, "Trust and obey, for there's no other way, to be happy in Jesus, but to trust and obey."[2] God resists the proud and gives grace to the humble (James 4:6).

Listening to the various popular atheists of the day, such as Richard

Dawkins, one observes tremendous anger on their part against God and any who believe in Him. For example, Dawkins says that God is "arguably the most unpleasant character in all fiction; a petty, unjust, unforgiving control-freak; a vindictive, bloodthirsty ethnic cleanser; a misogynistic homophobic, racist, infanticidal, genocidal, filicidal, pestilential, megalomaniacal, sadomasochistic, capriciously malevolent bully," a "psychotic delinquent," an "evil monster."[3] Anyone who doesn't share his belief in atheistic Darwinian evolution he calls "ignorant, stupid, or insane (or wicked, but I'd rather not consider that)."[4] I (Wayne) often have mused over why some should have so much anger against a being they believe doesn't exist. I think it is because they know that He exists and are angry because something did not go right for them in life, and He is an easy target for their anger.

Not everyone is angry at God, however. In the course of my research for this book, I came across a moving article on the Internet written by pastor Daryl Witmer. He was hospitalized for eight months with Guillain-Barré syndrome in 1984–85. He was afflicted by extensive paralysis and had great difficulty breathing. One Sunday morning he was wheeled to chapel with the help of a nurse who regularly pumped air into his lungs using an ambu (self-inflating) bag. He remembers little of the sermon and the preacher that morning, during which he struggled to breathe and to find some physical comfort while sitting in his wheelchair. What he does remember with considerable emotion, he said, are some words from a hymn that was sung that morning:

> Does Jesus care when my heart is pained
> Too deeply for mirth and song;
> As the burdens press and the cares distress,
> And the way grows weary and long?

Pastor Witmer said that he had led his past congregations in singing that song several times, but on that morning in the chapel, while he was experiencing great physical and emotional difficulty, the words met him in his time of need:

> O yes, He cares; I know He cares,
> His heart is touched with my grief;
> When the days are weary, the long nights dreary,
> I know my Savior cares. He cares.[5]

Witmer said these words dealt with the "core of the issue with which I had been struggling for weeks, and the truth they conveyed was far more therapeutic than all the medicine in the place."[6] Even in his pain this pastor knew with his heart what he no doubt had said with his mouth many times before—that God truly does have great care for us.

The God Who Empathizes with Our Pain

Does God feel our pain? This is a burning question for the one who is suffering under some financial, emotional, family, or physical burden. People in this predicament sense the need for support from anyone who will come to their aid, but particularly they desire support from God. Those who believe in a God, or those who have embraced the God of the Bible, know that He is capable of coming to their aid far better than any human. An interesting study reported on the Internet said that the majority of people believe more in the power of God to heal them than their physicians.[7]

Before answering whether God does in fact feel our pain, we must define what we mean by this statement. A president in the '90s often spoke about feeling people's pain, and considerable skepticism arose regarding the use of the phrase. Can anyone, even God, really feel our pain? To answer this, we must acknowledge that there is considerable difference between *knowing* of someone's pain and actually *feeling* someone's pain. Ravi Zacharias has rightly understood the difference:

> I never actually feel your pain. I am pained as I see you in pain. That is empathy. I am pained as I consider the matter that pains you. That is sympathy. In neither case do I feel your pain. Your pain is experienced by you, and my pain is experienced by me.[8]

So the question remains: Even though I (Wayne) may not feel your pain and you may not truly experience mine, is God able to feel it because He is God? We will explore this in the chapters to come.

Yet again, what it is that people want to know when they ask whether God feels their pain? They want to know whether God understands their problems, their suffering. And if He does, does He truly care about them? And if He truly cares, will He come to their aid? Then there's the matter of the believer being willing to trust God even if He should choose *not* to alleviate his or her suffering.

What's more, when we speak of God understanding and experiencing human pain, we must consider the way in which God entered into human history and human suffering and death through His Son (more on this in chapter 7). No one could watch the Mel Gibson movie *The Passion of the Christ* without being moved by the intense emotional, physical, and spiritual suffering endured by the Lord Jesus. A person might retort that many other people have endured much more suffering and more prolonged deaths than Jesus did. But what is not often understood is that the torment Jesus went through was far more than just physical. He suffered as the innocent one—unlike every other human, who deserves punishment due to their sins. Jesus chose to come into our fallen world having known perfect bliss in eternity (Philippians 2:5-8).

Something unique happened in the incarnation. The God who is transcendent above His creation became a part of His creation through the person of His Son. And the God who lives in perfect bliss without indecision, change, or the passions of mankind nonetheless became a suffering and dying Savior who truly understands our situation: "We do not have a High Priest who cannot sympathize with our weaknesses, but was in all points tempted as we are, yet without sin. Let us therefore come boldly to the throne of grace, that we may obtain mercy and find grace to help in time of need" (Hebrews 4:15-16).

When we examine the Old Testament text regarding God's acts on behalf of His people, we encounter the typical ways in which God works, finally epitomized in the sending His Son. We discover the true God and not some image of Him created in our own image. Moreover, as Hebrews 4:15-16 indicates, we too become involved in receiving the mercy and assistance of God. The issue is not whether we can change the mind of the eternal, unchangeable God. Few believe that God can be manipulated in this manner. Moreover, no biblically literate Christian believes that God needs and acts on our limited knowledge and wisdom, or may be pressured by us. Rather, we are called to embrace God's will for us and believe that God—from eternity past—has chosen to act through our prayers—within time—to sustain us when we falter, to forgive us when we sin, to heal us when we are physically or emotionally sick, and to comfort us when we are distraught.

Our comfort is to be found, then, when we encounter the clear teaching of Scripture about the compassion and love of God.

It is not difficult to understand how God, as presented by Jesus, has this attitude. Unfortunately, we are often led to believe that the God of the Old Testament is stern, distant, and aloof. Such is not the case, however, because there is but one God who is the God of the Bible. We need only to observe the way in which He presents Himself to His people to see that He is eternal and unchanging in His love, compassion, concern, and desire to meet their needs and longings consistent with what He has created them to be.

What we need to do, then, is really get to know the God of the Bible, rather than rely on our human perceptions or how He has been portrayed in movies, popular lore, or even in some churches. We must not seek to create Him as something other than He really is, for this is idolatry. And we must not think of Him as something less than He is, for then He is no longer God. That's why, in chapter 5, we will explore exactly who God is as portrayed in the Bible.

Chapter Two

Why All the Misery in the World?

❧

We live in a world filled with suffering, and that suffering is a consequence of sin (whether directly or indirectly). But it was not always this way. There was a time when there was no pain, no suffering whatsoever. In the Garden, Adam and Eve experienced perfection. Both they and the world around them did not experience hurt. In fact, God designed humans and indeed the whole creation to exist without pain.

God's Intention for Adam and Eve

Created in God's Image

Genesis 1:26 tells us that God created man in His image "according to Our likeness." In this way male and female were created in a perfect state, without decay or blemish. It is this great characteristic that sets man apart from the rest of creation. Man is the only creature to have been created this way. The word "image" is *tselem* in Hebrew, derived from the root word meaning "to cut or carve" and is used of an object carved to look like something else. The word "likeness" is *d'muth*, whose root means "to be like." We could say, then, that man is created "in an image which is like" God.

Theologians debate over what exactly this means, but as we will see from Genesis, it is clear that man is given dominion over the earth in a similar way that God has dominion over all things. Psalm 8 echoes this idea. David, having exalted God for the glory of His creation, says,

> What is man that You are mindful of him, and the son of man that You visit him? For You have made him a little lower than the angels, and You have crowned him with glory and honor. You have made him to have dominion over the works of Your hands; You have put all things under his feet, all sheep and oxen—even the beasts of the field, the birds of the air, and the fish of the sea that pass through the paths of the seas. O LORD, our Lord, how excellent is Your name in all the earth! (Psalm 8:6-9).

We may also say that because God created humans as individuals with their own personalities, God is personal (this attribute is discussed in chapter 5 as well). That is, He can be related to personally, not as pantheism argues (that God is everything, "the energy of the universe" or an impersonal force), but in a way that allows Adam and Eve to interact with Him. As we will see, it was God's intent to do so. Perhaps most important to our discussion here is that being created in God's image and likeness means man was given the ability to love and hate. This is not true of any other creature. Animals may seem to exhibit affection, but they cannot love. God intended man to love Him and love his neighbor with the same *kind* of love God Himself possesses.

When God gave His law to the people Israel He told them, "You shall love the LORD your God with all your heart, with all your soul, and with all your strength" (Deuteronomy 6:5). He also said, "You shall not take vengeance, nor bear any grudge against the children of your people, but you shall love your neighbor as yourself: I am the LORD" (Leviticus 19:18), and "The stranger who dwells among you shall be to you as one born among you, and you shall love him as yourself" (verse 34). He also intended us to hate. At first glance we may recoil at this thought, but we must keep in mind we're referring to a *biblical* definition of hate. We are to abhor evil in any form and hate sin. When the Lord was giving His final instructions to the Israelites before going into the Promised Land, He commanded them not to serve Him the way the Canaanites did. God said, "You shall not worship the LORD your God in that way; for every abomination to the LORD which He hates they have done to their gods; for they burn even their sons and daughters in the fire to their gods" (Deuteronomy 12:31). We too are to hate sin.

Created to Be Dependent on God

Adam and Eve, and indeed the entire creation, were created to be entirely dependent upon God, receiving their being from Him. The apostle Paul, presenting the gospel to the men of Athens, declared, "In Him we live and move and have our being, as also some of your own poets have said, 'For we are also His offspring'"(Acts 17:28). God intended for all creation, including the human race, not only to live in entire dependence upon Him but to acknowledge Him as the creator and sustainer of life. Nehemiah, in a great hymn of praise cried,

> Blessed be Your glorious name, which is exalted above all blessing and praise! You alone are the LORD; You have made heaven, the heaven of heavens, with all their host, the earth and everything on it, the seas and all that is in them, and You preserve them all. The host of heaven worships You (Nehemiah 9:5-6).

Not only were we designed to live in perfect dependency and acknowledgement of God as the sustainer of life, we were also intended to be His children. God intended Adam and Eve and all their offspring to be His offspring. We were to see God as our Father. The apostle Paul wrote, "Because you are sons, God has sent forth the Spirit of His Son into your hearts, crying out, 'Abba, Father!'" (Galatians 4:6-7). The apostle John, relating both God's love and our relationship to Him, cried, "Behold what manner of love the Father has bestowed on us, that we should be called children of God!" (1 John 3:1).

Created to Be Fruitful Stewards

God commanded Adam and Eve to "be fruitful and multiply; fill the earth and subdue it; have dominion over the fish of the sea, over the birds of the air, and over every living thing that moves on the earth" (Genesis 1:28). They were to be stewards of the earth, cooperating with animals and tending them. There is no indication that the taking of life was part of the original plan for Adam and Eve in the Garden, and it is thought that even carnivores ate plants in Eden (Genesis 1:30). God blessed Adam and Eve, giving them everything they needed to live so they would never experience want. He said, "Behold, I have given you every plant yielding seed that is on the face of all the earth, and every tree with seed in its fruit. You shall have them for food" (Genesis 1:29 ESV).

Adam was put in Eden to "tend and keep" it (Genesis 2:15). In fact the very word "Eden" means "delight." When God had finished His work of creation, seeing "everything He had made," He saw that "it was very good." The descendants of Adam and Eve were never to experience the hardships of life, strife, war, hunger, thirst, depression, rage, disability, or disease. Humanity was never to experience evil in any form. It was God's intention for Adam and Eve to be the progenitors of humanity, to live in this perfect world forever.

Intended for Fellowship

It was God's intention for humans never to experience loneliness or solitude. After God created Adam, it was clear than none of the other living creatures could relate to Adam or function as his partner in Eden. So God created Eve, Adam's helpmate. Bible commentator Matthew Henry beautifully illustrates God's plan for Adam and Eve's relationship. He noted

> that the woman was *made of a rib out of the side of Adam;* not made out of his head to rule over him, nor out of his feet to be trampled upon by him, but out of his side to be equal with him, under his arm to be protected, and near his heart to be beloved.[1]

Thus it was also God's intention for Adam and Eve to enjoy close, personal relationship with God. Humans were never to have been estranged from God. In Genesis when God is said to be "walking in the garden in the cool of the day" (Genesis 3:8), it is believed this was a regular occurrence, and that Adam and Eve possibly had intimate conversations with God. Eden was to be a place where man and God would enjoy fellowship together for eternity. There would be no separation from God, no eternal punishment for sin, and no death to end life in Eden.

The Nature of the Fall of Humanity

However, God gave Adam and Eve this command: "Of every tree of the garden you may freely eat; but the tree of the knowledge of good and evil you shall not eat, for in the day that you eat of it you shall surely die" (Genesis 2:16-17). This was the first prohibition recorded in the Bible and the only one Adam and Eve were under. Unfortunately for them, the rest of God's creation, and all humanity to follow, they did not keep this command, and ever since then, human misery has been the result.

The Fateful Conversation

The Bible recounts how the serpent, who was "more cunning than any beast of the field" (and was acting on behalf of or was possessed by Satan) comes to Eve. He questions her: "Has God indeed said, 'You shall not eat of every tree of the garden'?"(Genesis 3:1). The mistake was deliberate, designed to get Eve to question God in her own mind. She should have never talked with the serpent. In fact, it was improper for the serpent to do this to Eve given God's command that Adam and Eve have dominion over animals. Instead, she tries to answer the serpent and incorrectly quotes the original command: "We may eat the fruit of the trees of the garden; but of the fruit of the tree which is in the midst of the garden, God has said, 'You shall not eat it, nor shall you touch it, lest you die'" (Genesis 3:2-3).

In her response, Eve forgets the words "any" and "freely,"

de-emphasizing God's graciousness, and adds the prohibition of even touching the fruit, incorrectly making God more legalistic. Further, she omitted the phrase "in the day that you eat of it you shall surely," downplaying the immediacy of punishment and God's faithfulness in carrying out what He says He will do. The cunning serpent senses Eve's weakness and continues his argument, accusing God of lying to her and Adam to protect Himself. The serpent tells Eve, "You will not surely die," and committing a logical fallacy, he continues, "For God knows that in the day you eat of it your eyes will be opened, and you will be like God, knowing good and evil" (Genesis 3:5). In other words, "God won't kill you if you disobey His command. He knows if you eat the fruit of this tree you will become like Him."

The serpent insinuates that God had withheld something from Adam and Eve, and that they were somehow incomplete without this knowledge. Often, incompleteness is equated with imperfection. Adam and Eve, according to the serpent's argument, were imperfect, and the serpent seems to argue that the unjust denial of the wisdom provided by this fruit was causing them suffering.

The Fall

The desire for this wisdom proves so powerful that Eve gives into the temptation to eat of the one tree forbidden by God. Then Adam also took and ate the fruit. As God promised, Adam and Eve died that day, though not physically (which was the lie that the serpent had convinced them of). The moment they ate, they died spiritually and became imperfect, subject to decay. God told Adam, "In the sweat of your face you shall eat bread, till you return to the ground, for out of it you were taken; for dust you are, and to dust you shall return" (Genesis 3:19). Adam and Eve were cast out of Eden, doomed to live the rest of their days working for their living and experiencing pain. God tells Adam, "Cursed is the ground because of you; in pain you shall eat of it all the days of your life; thorns and thistles it shall bring forth for you; and you shall eat the plants of the field" (Genesis 3:17-18 ESV).

Anyone who has ever raised a crop or tried their hand at vegetable gardening knows the labor and pain involved in trying to get plants to produce food. No longer would Adam and Eve be given sustenance from the plants of Eden. Also, God tells Eve, "I will surely multiply your pain in childbearing; in pain you shall bring forth children" (Genesis 3:16 ESV). Any mother will tell you the pain of childbirth is excruciating. God goes on, "Your desire shall be for [or against] your husband, and he shall rule over you" (Genesis 3:16 ESV). From this point on, there would be strife between men and women. The perfect happiness Adam and Eve experienced as a husband and wife would forever be lost.

It was at this time sin entered creation and would remain at the heart of human suffering. The apostle Paul wrote, "Just as through one man sin entered the world, and death through sin, and thus death spread to all men, because all sinned..." (Romans 5:12; 1 Corinthians 15:22). He goes on to say that the judgment that came as a result of Adam's sin resulted in condemnation, and from Adam's disobedience, men were made sinners. Indeed, man's own nature became enslaved to sin (Romans 6:6). No longer would Adam and Eve be permitted to remain in God's presence in Eden. Rather, they would live separated from Him.

The Impact of Sin on Our Relationships

Sin's Impact in the Beginning

Almost immediately in the Genesis account we see the impact of sin on our relationship with God, others, and ourselves. In Genesis 4 the sons of Adam, Cain and Abel, bring their offerings to the Lord. Abel, a "keeper of sheep," brings his firstborn of the flock, while Cain brings an offering of "the fruit of the ground" (verses 3-4). While theologians debate about the significance of the offerings, what is clear is that Cain's offering was somehow inferior. It seems to be that while Abel offered a great sacrifice, giving to God the first blessings of his labor, Cain held something back from God. Cain seems to be unwilling to worship God correctly, and in turn, God rejects Cain's offering. Cain reacts to God's rejection in anger, prompting a warning from God: "Why are you angry? And why has your countenance fallen? If you do well, will you not be accepted? And if you do not do well, sin lies at the door. And its desire is for you, but you should rule over it" (Genesis 4:6-7).

The issue here is not that anger is sin. Rather, it's what we become angry for, and what anger causes us to do. In his anger Cain murdered Abel, then flippantly lied about it to God and received the punishment of being cursed to wander the earth as a vagabond instead of raising crops.

Here we see that sin affected Cain's relationship with God. Cain's sinful attitude caused his worship to be rejected by God. We also see how sin affects our relationships with each other. Abel did nothing to deserve being killed; the murder was entirely Cain's problem with God. Yet Abel experienced the ultimate form of suffering—death. Finally, we see here the effect sin has on ourselves. Cain forever suffered the fate of wandering the earth, scavenging for his survival—surely not a pleasant existence. In fact, God put a mark on Cain so that Cain himself would not be murdered.

Sin's Impact Today

Every day, sin affects us. The bliss that was the Garden of Eden, and the perfect creation Adam and Eve enjoyed and all their descendants were to participate in, was inevitably changed. In the previous chapter we mentioned how natural disasters inflict suffering upon humanity. They are among the effects of sin. All the failings of human life began with Adam's disobedience.

To this day, our relationship with God is broken because of sin. Unless we have faith in Jesus as our Savior, that relationship will never be repaired. We will live our lives separated from God, lacking a relationship with Him. We will live in despair, vainly searching for meaning in life. And even after we become Christians, sin can hinder our fellowship with God. We may give in to our sinful desires and refuse to worship Him properly. Or, we may blame God for our suffering instead of running to Him for help.

Sin also effects our relationships with others. We may refuse to fellowship with others due to selfishness. We may lash out at those whom we love most because we are angry at something else. In our sin we lie to, cheat, steal from, and hurt those around us.

Sin may also cause us to hurt ourselves. Sometimes sin feels good. It brings momentary pleasure, but the end result is detrimental—either physically, mentally, or spiritually. Sin causes men to do unspeakable evil to one another, from oppression to tyranny, from murder to mass executions. These behaviors are a direct result of sin.

The Impact of Sin and the Fallen Creation

Suffering Caused by Natural Disasters

Perhaps no other recent natural disaster better depicts the fallen state of the world than the events surrounding Hurricane Katrina, which wreaked destruction upon Gulf Coast states in August 2005. As of this writing, it is almost exactly three years after the catastrophe, and the city of New Orleans is far from recovered. The human suffering caused by Hurricane Katrina covers a broad spectrum of causes, regardless of one's political views. Before, during, and after the hurricane, the fallen nature and sinfulness of man were both on vivid display.

The city of New Orleans lies on a floodplain at the mouth of the Mississippi River, and has an average elevation of only five feet above sea level. Its highest point is fifteen feet above sea level, while some areas of the city are five feet below sea level. Because of offshore erosion, the city is actually sinking. It is estimated that within 90 years, the entire city will be below sea level. Because most of New Orleans is below sea level, levees and dikes were built for the purpose of protecting the city from flooding by the Mississippi River and the waters in the Gulf of Mexico. Despite the precarious setting, almost 470,000 people lived in New Orleans.

In August 2005, Hurricane Katrina marched across the Gulf of Mexico and headed toward New Orleans. Mayor Ray Nagin was warned that this powerful storm would most likely breach the levees and flood most of the city. Yet he hesitated in ordering an evacuation, allegedly because he was worried that tourist interests would sue the city for disrupting commerce.

In the end, Nagin and Governor Kathleen Blanco did not order a mandatory evacuation until 19 hours before the storm made landfall. Even if they had ordered an evacuation in time, many of the city's poor had no way to leave, not having access to cars. No plans were made beforehand for evacuating those who could not leave on their own. Instead, Nagin and other officials urged residents to come to the Superdome, what he called the "shelter of last resort." There was little attempt to supply this "shelter" with provisions. In fact, Nagin asked citizens to bring their own supplies. By the afternoon of August 28, 26,000 people had come to the Superdome. In the end, more than 70,000 people did not evacuate the city.

At 11:00 AM August 29, Katrina slammed into New Orleans. Within hours, as predicted (but unheeded), overflow and breaches in the city's levee system caused the flooding of 80 percent of the city, with water 20 feet deep in some places. Many residents who chose to stay or could not leave were stranded in their homes. Some took refuge on their roofs, while others were trapped and perished in their attics as they attempted to get above the rising waters.

Even after the storm passed, the floodwaters remained, leaving New Orleans with no clean water. Boats or helicopters were the only means of getting around in the city. Because of the flooding and lack of preparation, there was no way to efficiently evacuate the refugees who had fled to the Superdome and other areas of higher ground. Buses that could have been used to evacuate the city before the storm sat empty for lack of drivers, or because they were now flooded. Law and order completely disintegrated due to the police being overwhelmed by numerous search and rescue duties, officers simply fleeing, or worse, officers defecting and engaging in illegal activity themselves. There were even reports of rescue helicopters being shot at. Although the exact number of fatalities is unknown, at least 1500 people died during Katrina and its aftermath.

The way that people acted during the storm and its aftermath shows how sin affects human life on many levels. As mentioned, simply living in our fallen world can lead to suffering. Natural disasters like Katrina are a result of the fall of man and rejection of God's provision. Katrina showed no discrimination as it inflicted pain and suffering on people. Simply being in New Orleans in August 2005 was the criteria for experiencing the storm. Tens of thousands lost their homes and possessions due to the flooding. Even though some years have passed, the damage caused by the storm is still being repaired. Some areas have simply been abandoned.

On a more personal level, however (and regardless of one's politics), it is clear that human failing directly led to human suffering. Governmental planning was woefully lacking. Because there were no plans in place for evacuating those who could not leave on their own, tens of thousands suffered, while many suffered the ultimate fate of death. Government officials may have allowed economic concerns to overshadow concern for people's lives. Whatever the reason, the failure to order mandatory evacuations led to unneeded deaths. Leah Hodges, a survivor of the storm, pointed out ironically that "[t]he stray animals from the animal shelter, most of whom would have been euthanized, were evacuated two days before the storm, and the people were left to die. Buses that could have gotten our people, who otherwise could not get out were left to flood, and people were left to die."[2]

Conspiracy theories aside, the levees that were supposed to protect from flooding failed, and it is becoming increasingly clear that human error contributed to the failure. Raymond Seed of the University of California, Berkeley stated, "...we're receiving some very disturbing reports from people who were involved in some of these projects, and it suggests that perhaps not just human error was involved; there may have been some malfeasance. Some of the sections may not have been constructed as they were designed."[3] There may also be evidence of corruption on the part of some of the officials involved in the levees' construction. Someone's sinful actions led to the suffering and even deaths of many people.

And, after the storm, the rampant lawlessness that broke out all over the city put man's sinful nature on vivid display. Many New Orleans citizens engaged in stealing whatever they could find. Assaults, rapes, and murders became common. In fact, there were reports of police officers participating in the chaos.[4] Human suffering was directly caused by the sinful actions of other humans.

All of what happened with Hurricane Katrina and afterward is one example of how people suffer as a result of nature's wrath, human error, and sinful actions that inflict harm upon others.

Suffering Caused by Our Sinful Nature

Suffering caused by the sinfulness of the human condition is unfortunately becoming more and more prevalent in our world. Theodore Dalrymple, a medical doctor who has practiced in Third World countries and British prisons, has commented extensively on the subject. Over and over again he recounts how destructive behaviors lead to the suffering of men and women on an almost unimaginable scale. For the most part, their suffering is either self-caused or a result of not taking steps to protect themselves from suffering at the hands of others.

For example, Dalrymple recounts the story of a 17-year-old patient admitted to his ward with acute alcohol poisoning. She confessed to Dalrymple that she had been a heavy drinker since age 12. What was the reason for her current binge? A personal crisis. Her boyfriend had been sentenced to detention for a series of burglaries and assaults, and she could not bear the thought of being apart from him for a few months. Her mother was also an alcoholic with "a taste for violent boyfriends."[5] When Dalrymple tried to warn her that the choices she was making might end up getting her hurt or worse, she replied, "I can look after myself." When he pointed out that in general men are physically stronger than women and so are at an advantage when it comes to physical violence, she accused him of sexism. She refused to acknowledge that her actions were destructive, choosing instead to attack the one person trying to save her.

Sadly, this kind of attitude is pervasive in our world. Dalrymple recounts another story of another young woman who had overdosed on drugs after her ex-boyfriend broke down the front door of her apartment, smashed the place, broke all the windows, stole cash, and ripped the phone out of the wall. Over the four years she had been with him, he had broken her thumb, ribs, and jaw, and hit her in the face multiple times. When Dalrymple asked why she had stayed with this man and had two children by him, she could only say, "It's complicated, doctor. That's the way life goes sometimes."[6] She attributed her situation to unalterable circumstances out of her control.

One may wonder why there is so much suffering in our world today. In many cases, we need look no further than our own sinfulness. Unfortunately, modern psychology has done a thorough job of convincing us that our suffering is a result of something other than our own actions, as illustrated above. The 17-year-old focused on Dalrymple's perceived sexism rather than acknowledging her behavior as the cause of her suffering. The other woman, who had endured multiple beatings, simply didn't "want to think about it" and was more concerned about the government moving her to a new residence after the old one was destroyed. In later chapters, we will discuss further the implications of suffering, even that pain can be beneficial; but we must remember that much of our misery is self-inflicted, derived from our own sinful nature and living in a fallen and sinful world.

God Is Not the Cause of the Fall

We must keep in mind while discussing Adam's sin that it was Adam's actions, not God's, that were the cause of the fall. Adam was free to make the choice he did. God did not force Adam and Eve to disobey Him. God is not a rigid determinative deity who directly causes all actions and events; therefore, God is not morally responsible for the origin of pain and suffering. It is, as we noted from the apostle Paul, Adam's sin that brought death to humanity. In chapter 3 we will discuss the issue of theodicy (why God allows evil), but for now it's sufficient to say God allowed Adam to make the decision to disobey and sin, and that ultimately paved the way for the introduction of pain into the world.

God's Promise of a Glorious Future

We have seen that suffering was not an original intention of God. He created a perfect world for Adam and Eve and their descendants—a world free from pain, whether physical, mental, or spiritual. Unfortunately, Adam and Eve gave in to temptation and fell from their perfect state, and sin entered God's perfect creation. The presence of sin in the world led to the presence of pain and suffering. Adam was forced to toil for his sustenance, and Eve would feel great pain in childbirth. Cain murdered Abel because he was angry with God. Abel suffered death, while Cain suffered the consequences of his actions. And the effects of sin have continued to be manifest since. Today we suffer at the hands of this fallen world. Sin causes us to be estranged from God. We fail to worship Him, sometimes even running from Him or hating Him, causing spiritual suffering. Sin causes us to do horrendous things to each other, even ourselves, as we saw in the examples recounted by Dalrymple.

Fortunately, we are not forever doomed to suffering. Praise God, He did not abandon us to our deserved fate! Instead, He provided us with hope—He has promised of a coming time when His creation will be restored and all those who are His children will live for eternity in a new heaven and new earth. The prophet Isaiah recorded the Lord's promise:

> For behold, I create new heavens and a new earth; and the former shall not be remembered or come to mind. But be glad and rejoice forever in what I create…I will rejoice in Jerusalem, and joy in My people; the voice of weeping shall no longer be heard in her, nor the voice of crying (Isaiah 65:17-19).

The apostle Peter looks forward to that day, saying, "We, according to His promise, look for new heavens and a new earth in which righteousness dwells" (2 Peter 3:13). And Jesus Himself, through the apostle John, gives us this promise:

Now I saw a new heaven and a new earth, for the first heaven and the first earth had passed away. Also there was no more sea. Then I, John, saw the holy city, New Jerusalem, coming down out of heaven from God, prepared as a bride adorned for her husband. And I heard a loud voice from heaven saying, "Behold, the tabernacle of God is with men, and He will dwell with them, and they shall be His people. God Himself will be with them and be their God. And God will wipe away every tear from their eyes; there shall be no more death, nor sorrow, nor crying. There shall be no more pain, for the former things have passed away."

Then He who sat on the throne said, "Behold, I make all things new" (Revelation 21:1-5).

What a glorious future to look forward to! We cannot help but repeat John's words, crying, "Amen. Even so, come, Lord Jesus!" (Revelation 22:20).

Chapter Three

Why Has God Allowed
Evil in the World?

Pain and suffering are real. They are not mere states of mind or mirages. And we have seen that sin is to blame for evil, not God. We have also seen that God is good and loving. How do we solve the perceived contradictions between these truths? How can God be perfect and all-powerful, yet seemingly unable or unwilling to put a stop to evil? How can God be said to be good and loving, yet allow sin and all its consequences?

In two of the examples mentioned earlier, the tsunamis in the Indian Ocean and Hurricane Katrina, hundreds of thousands of people lost their lives. Was God powerless or unwilling to stop these catastrophes? Why does He allow the suffering of so many?

These questions fall in the realm of theology known today as *theodicy*. While philosophers have for centuries debated the existence and causes of evil, the actual term *theodicy* is generally credited to G.W. Leibniz and dates to about 1710. Leibniz attempted to reconcile the seeming contradictions mentioned above, and many have followed in his footsteps. Atheists frequently raise these same questions to "prove" God does not exist. Others use them to show that Christians have a wrong view of the God of the Bible. Many others use the questions as an excuse to rebel against God.

In this chapter we will focus on the question, Why has God allowed evil in the world? While the issues relating to the problem of evil can involve highly complex theological and philosophical arguments, we will summarize the key points here as clearly and succinctly as possible.

Insufficient Attempts to Resolve the Problem

While many religions believe in God, most have not adequately addressed the problem of evil. Instead, they simply deny one or more of God's attributes. For example, deists deny God's omniscience (the fact He is all-knowing). They say God created the world (perfect or not) and left it to its own devices. Others deny God's omnipotence (all-powerfulness) and say there is a great cosmic battle between good and evil. God is good, and Satan is evil, and the two are duking it out in a cosmic contest of wills. The two sides are roughly equal in strength, so the battle will go on until Armageddon, when God finally triumphs over Satan and evil. This view seems to be popular among Hollywood filmmakers, who constantly release films depicting such conflict (and, as we all know, the good guys always, or at least usually, win).

Still others argue a more moderate position. God, they say, isn't all-powerful or all-knowing. He is, rather, *very* powerful and *very* wise. This is known as the Free Will view, or Open Theism. In order to protect humanity's freedom of decision, Open Theists see God as cooperating with people, perhaps nudging them toward what He wishes. In His wise state, God has a plan for our ultimate benefit, but He is also able to adapt and change according to our actions. In the end, evil is a result of humans failing to choose God and His ways, and unfortunately, God cannot ultimately stop us from doing it. Open Theism has (correctly) been criticized for making God into some kind of benevolent gambler who hopes that people make the right decisions and is powerless to stop them from making wrong decisions. This view, however, does not explain why seemingly innocent people, through no decision of their own, experience pain and suffering. At the other end of the religious spectrum is Islam. As one Muslim philosopher puts it,

"What strikes you was not there to miss you; what misses you was not there to strike you."[1] There is no contradiction for Islam because Allah determines all things, whether good or evil, and to question the actions of Allah is to show a lack of faith, to fail to submit to him, which is the ultimate sin (*Muslim* means "one who submits").

Ultimately for Islam, humans live under the fate that God has decreed for them, with no possibility of escape. To the Muslim, God is so beyond human understanding and so infinitely sovereign that we cannot possibly understand why he does what he does. He is neither good nor bad, he is simply Allah. Islam answers the question of human suffering by saying, "Because." In the end, the argument dissolves into circular reasoning:

> Why is there evil?
> Because Allah wills it.
> Why does Allah will it?
> Because he is Allah.

Some Islamic thinkers have at times attempted to give a better answer than that. They say that if humans did not know hardship, they would not recognize abundance. If humans did not know pain, they would not know what pleasure is, and so on. While this may be true on the surface, it is logically incorrect to say that good cannot be known without evil. This does not answer the contradiction posed between the belief that Allah decides all things, yet man's purpose in life is to submit to Allah. Either Allah decides man's actions, whether good or evil, or Allah doesn't decide all things and man is free to act, and the question of evil remains unanswered.

Improper Perspectives of God and Evil

Does the Presence of Evil Mean God Is Not Perfect?

In answer to that question, we must first deal with the objection that a perfect God would not have made a world in which evil could exist. The usual argument goes something like this:

A perfect being can create only that which is perfect.
The world is not perfect.
God created the world.
Therefore, God is not perfect.

This line of reasoning is advocated by several philosophies. Those with a *pantheistic* worldview believe this. Pantheism teaches that God is everything and everything is God. Rather than a distinct being, God is referred to as "Unity." Our world, then, is tied to God's existence, so that whatever exists has the attributes of this Unity. Since the world is not perfect, the universal force existing in all things that they call God is not perfect either. In fact, most pantheists accept that both good and evil exist in the Unity, and some more radical pantheists (those in the New Age movement) fall into believing that evil is a state of mind or a failure to realize unity with the Unity.

Some traditional theists also hold this view. For them, God is the "most perfect Being possible," so everything He produces also must be the most perfect possible. As we have seen, God *did* create a perfect world. It was Adam's actions that introduced imperfection into the world. But both of these views deny the Garden of Eden and the fall of man accounts in the Bible as true historical events, so they are forced to construct elaborate philosophies to account for the existence of evil. Ultimately, they arrive at the unbiblical view that God is not perfect. So then the next logical question is this: Does the presence of evil mean that God is not perfect?

Deists claim that God is not perfect because He is unaware of some things. God did not know Adam would sin and introduce evil into the creation. In fact, God is said to have created the universe, then left it to its own devices.

There is, however, no reason to believe God was unaware of what Adam would do and the consequences of sin in the world. Further, the Bible clearly shows that God does interact with His creation. He was fully aware of what Adam would do. So the presence of evil was known to Him in eternity. It did not come as a surprise.

Open Theism says God is a learning being who is capable of mistakes. He can and does change in reaction to human actions. The presence of evil in the world, then, is a mistake on God's part. In His great wisdom, God predicted Adam would probably fall, but did not know for sure. He took a chance and created Adam anyway. In this way, Open Theists attempt to absolve God from the discussion of evil. He simply hoped Adam would not sin. This view, in essence, denies that God is God. It makes Him into *a god,* rather than *the God.* The God of the Bible becomes one of the many gods of the world's religions, no better than Baal, Zeus, Krishna, or one of the hundreds of thousands of gods in Hinduism.

This will not do, however, because the Bible portrays God as the Lord of the universe, before whom there are no other gods. In Deuteronomy God says, "Now see that I, even I, am He, and there is no god besides Me" (32:39). Solomon, in 1 Kings, affirms, "the LORD is God; there is no other" (8:60). He is unique, not one of many. Clearly, God alone is to be worshipped. If the presence of evil means God is not perfect, He cannot be said to be God as we know Him from Scripture.

Does the Presence of Evil Mean God Is Not All-Powerful?

This question has to do with God's *omnipotence,* or His all-powerful nature. There are some who argue that God cannot be all-powerful, because evil exists. David Hume, one of the most famous philosophers of the nineteenth century, posed this argument: If God is willing to prevent evil but is not able, then He is impotent. And if He is able but not willing, then He is malevolent.[2] Surely God would stop suffering and pain if it were in His power to do so.

Alternate Explanations Regarding Good and Evil

Open Theism

The conclusion of many is that God, even if He wanted to stop evil, is powerless to do so. Such is the view of some Open Theists. They see the freedom of man as such a powerful force that God can do nothing to thwart it (without man ceasing to be free). God is bound by our freedom not to intervene against evil. Open Theists point to the example of Adam and Eve as proving this. God could have stopped them from sinning but did not because He could not violate their freedom. This view denies God's sovereignty. While the debate over free will continues in theological circles, none but the Open Theists would give man this much power.

But the mere fact God doesn't actively stop evil doesn't mean He is unable to do so. Many atheists see through this argument and correctly point out that a non-all-powerful God is no God at all (though they then continue onward to the wrong assumption that there is no God). In truth, there are many passages of Scripture that show God is in control of all things, even the choices of man. For example, Isaiah 14:24 says, "The LORD of hosts has sworn, saying, 'Surely, as I have thought, so it shall come to pass, and as I have purposed, so it shall stand.'" While God does allow human freedom, this does not mean God is not omnipotent.[3]

Rabbi Kushner

Rabbi Harold Kushner came to the conclusion that God is not all-powerful after watching his son die of progeria, a rare genetic disorder that causes the body to age rapidly. Kushner's son never grew more than three feet tall, and died at age 14. Kushner calls this his biggest disappointment in life, and it destroyed his original view of God. In response to what happened to his son, Kushner began to examine the world around him. He saw unimaginable suffering everywhere. Gradually he began to try to reconcile the things he knew about God and the world he observed. He explains, "I believe in God. But I do not believe the same things about Him that I did years ago, when I was growing up or when I was a theological student. I recognize His limitations."[4] He continues,

> I grew up believing in an all-powerful God. But we
> have to tie ourselves in such knots to explain why an

omnipotent God permitted the Holocaust, why an omnipotent God permits children to be born retarded, why an omnipotent God permits earthquakes and hurricanes. It just got so complicated, you ended up twisted in so many theological knots, that it became unsustainable. There are two things in life that God does not control: one is laws of nature and the other is human choice. This does not diminish God. I would rather worship a God who is completely good but not totally powerful than a God who is completely powerful but not completely good.[5]

Rabbi Kushner's belief is the same as that of the philosopher David Hume: An all-powerful God cannot be all good, and an all-good God cannot be all powerful. Kushner felt he had to choose between the two. He says, "I can worship a God who hates suffering but cannot eliminate it, more easily than I can worship a God who chooses to make children suffer and die, for whatever exalted reason."[6] He has come to the conclusion that "God does not cause our misfortunes. Some are caused by bad luck, some are caused by bad people, and some are simply an inevitable consequence of our being human and being mortal, living in a world of inflexible natural laws."[7]

Kushner formerly thought that God would bless him because he was a "good man" who always tried to do right and carry out God's work. Believing he and his family were good, he thought God *could not* punish him or his family. When his son was diagnosed as having progeria, he could not reconcile why he had a sick son while so many obviously bad people had healthy children. We would not presume that God was punishing Kushner, but we also cannot limit what God chooses to do, for whatever reason.

In the Bible, we see David and Bathsheba's infant child experience the *consequence* of David's sin—he died (2 Samuel 12:15-19), though we are not suggesting that God directly *caused* the child to suffer because of David's sin. Instead of becoming angry with God or thinking God could not control what was happening, David reacted in faith: "Who can tell whether the LORD will be gracious to me, that the child may live?" (2 Samuel 12:22).

To place the requirement that suffering *cannot* be a punishment from God is to unjustifiably limit Him. Kushner assumed God does not punish sin with pain and tragedy, so these are things God cannot control. He argues, "The painful things that happen to us are not punishments for our misbehavior, nor are they in any way part of some grand design on God's part. Because the tragedy is not God's will, we need not feel hurt or betrayed by God when tragedy strikes."[8] Kushner has decided that God is frustrated by tragedy as much as we are, and that He is as powerless as we are to stop it. Kushner sees God as not being in control of all things, yet we can run to Him in times of distress for comfort. He says, "We can turn to Him for help in overcoming it, precisely because we can tell ourselves that God is as outraged by it as we are."[9] Viewed this way, God loses His divine attributes, becoming nothing more than a spiritual security blanket. Why would we find comfort in a God who can do nothing to alleviate suffering and can give no promise to end suffering?

While we would never presume to know the personal pain Kushner went through when he lost his son, we would also never want human experience to define God. As a transcendent being, God is not subject to our desires. As finite and imperfect humans we may desire a world without disease, hunger, famine, war, natural disasters, and the like, and we may desire a God who does not allow such things to happen. But believing God is unable to stop the bad things in life is wrong. To do so is to see God and judge Him through the finite, fallen, and imperfect lens of human understanding.

The fact that bad things *do* happen to good people in no way means God is not omnipotent. Moreover, a God who is unable to stop pain because He is bound "by laws of nature and by the evolution of human nature and human moral freedom" is no comfort to us. In the end we are without hope with this type of deity. If our God cannot provide even the promise of an end to suffering, why worship or even believe in Him? It would be like asking a patient to trust a surgeon who has just told him he is unable to perform the surgery the patient needs.

Baruch Spinoza

The philosophy of Baruch (Benedict) Spinoza (1632–1677), sometimes called *pantheistic determinism,* also denies God's omnipotence. Spinoza believed that God was not contingent, but necessary. In other words, God must exist (which is true). He does not depend on anything for His being, and there is no possibility He could not exist. Spinoza also rightly said that God is perfect (otherwise He could not be said to be God). So far, so good. But Spinoza also believed that "whatever is, is in God." He argued that whatever makes God "God" could not be separated from what God creates. God could not make something separate from Himself (we will discuss the implications of this logic in a moment).

Combining these two arguments, Spinoza said that whatever comes from God must be like God in every way. So God's creation *must exist* in the same way God *must exist.* God was not free to not create the world. It was not God's decision to create the world. God was forced by *necessity,* not His own will, to create the world. God, as well as everything in creation, is dictated by this "necessity." However, Spinoza never proved that God, being perfect, *needed* to create. It does not follow that a perfect God *must* create. It was by God's own will that He determined to create. In Revelation 4:11 we see this praise directed to God: "You are worthy, O Lord, to receive glory and honor and power; for You created all things, and by Your will they exist and were created."

Spinoza also failed to prove his pantheism. When a painter creates a work of art, the painter, by necessity, is not part of the painting. Much more so the eternal God is not part of his noneternal creation, for then He would become noneternal Himself. God, as infinite, cannot be part of a finite creation, and vice versa. If it is not true that everything exists "in God," then Spinoza's argument that things cannot be separate from God is false. Spinoza argued that the creation *flowed* from God's being, so must have the *exact* same qualities as God. But this is not so.

The God of the Bible clearly created something separate from Himself. As we saw above, God is infinite, while creation is finite. God is eternal, while creation is temporal (subject to time). Further, the Bible teaches that humans have some of the attributes of God, but not to the same extent as God. Humans have love, but not infinite love (1 John 4:8). Humans can be just, but not perfectly just (Isaiah 45:21). Humans can show mercy, but are not infinitely merciful (Psalm 116:5).

"A Good God Would Not Allow Evil"

The argument is often, "A good God would not allow evil." Those who say this see the immense amount of human suffering taking place on a daily basis and conclude that either there is no God or that God is not good. How could a being who is powerful enough to stop evil not do so?

SPINOZA'S "GOODNESS"

Spinoza believed God is all-powerful, for only an all-powerful God could have created the universe. But he avoided David Hume's conclusion that God must be malevolent if he is all-powerful by denying God's goodness. Spinoza thought that God was not good as we think of it, nor are things in the world good or evil. Because of his pantheism, Spinoza thought God was not a personal being who possessed discernible qualities. The things we deem good and evil are a result of our own perception of them, rather than some quality within the things themselves. In this way Spinoza thought he was negating the problem of evil, but he was actually *denying* the reality of evil. Also, the reason something is good or evil is not because we perceive it as such, but because God has told us what is good and evil. Things *do* in fact have inherent qualities. Sin is evil; God is good. These truths do not depend on our perception, nor do they change if we change.

WHAT IS "GOOD"?

We also need to discuss the definition of *good*. Because this definition changes greatly depending upon whom you ask, it would seem that humans aren't a very good source for determining the meaning of *good*. For example, it would be wrong, as we will see in later chapters, to assume that good always involves the absence of pain and suffering. Sometimes pain and suffering are for our benefit. For people to look at all the suffering in the world and conclude that there must be no good God is a failure of perspective. A better definition is that *good* means "something beneficial." In this way God can be said to be good, because He is always and infinitely beneficial.

Sin, Human Freedom, and God's Justice

Earlier, we saw that sin, which is the root cause of evil, came into the world through *human* failing, not God's. When God created Adam and Eve, they were created without the knowledge of good and evil. Not until they ate of the tree of the knowledge of good and evil did they know sin. There are some who would say that giving this option to Adam and Eve was not good. Apparently for them, *not* giving Adam and Eve freedom of choice would have been good. And it follows that for God to give freedom of choice to humans is *not* good. They would prefer that we were robots, preprogrammed to do good and not evil.

Ultimately, this view violates several principles. Firstly, God created humans with the capacity to act. He did not create robots built for the mere purpose of complying with His commands without thought or emotion. And, if God were simply to bring an end to evil today, it would violate His expression of justice. A God who is unjust could not be said to be good. What we are experiencing now is a direct result of our sin. God gave Adam and Eve the conditions for living in the Garden of Eden, and they violated them. God is good, but He is also just. Would we call a judge good if he dismissed the sentence against every guilty criminal who came before him so that the criminal would not suffer from his punishment? We would hope not. But why would we think this true of earthly judges dealing with criminals and yet doubt that God is good because He does not erase the just punishment for humanity's sin?

Does the Presence of Evil Mean God Is Not Loving?

DEFINING LOVE

One of God's attributes is that He is all-loving. As the Bible says, "God is love" (1 John 4:8). This is distinct from God being good. God could be good without being loving. To love is not necessarily to be good. For example, if a husband falls in love with a woman who is not his wife, that is not good. It is also possible for a good deed to lack the quality of love. We may say it is good to obey the speed limit, but that doesn't mean we love obeying it.

There are people who say that God cannot be all-loving because He allows evil, sin, pain, and suffering. Even some who acknowledge that God is omnipotent will nevertheless say that God is not all-loving because He does not stop evil even though He has the power to do it. And then there are those who say, "A God who condemns people to eternal suffering is not a God of love." But this argument flounders on the rocks of a wrong definition of love. Any view that says God is unloving comes from a wrong view of love.

LOVE, EVIL, AND GOD

It was God's love for mankind that led Him to give His Son to die on the cross on our behalf. So, can we define *love* as simply an absence of pain and suffering? Can we elevate the attribute of love above any other of God's attributes?

For the answers, we need look no further than a parent disciplining a child. In one way or another, all discipline is painful and results in the child suffering. From the child's perspective, the parent who dispenses discipline may seem unloving. Yet the very reason most parents discipline their children is because they love their children and want to raise them the right way.

Indeed, Scripture teaches, "He who spares his rod hates his son, but he who loves him disciplines him promptly" (Proverbs 13:24). In fact, Scriptures teach that *despite* human evil and sin, God loves us. Almost everyone is familiar with John 3:16: "God so loved the world that He gave His only begotten Son, that whoever believes in Him should not perish but have everlasting life." Paul further clarifies this love: "God demonstrates His own love toward us, in that while we were still sinners, Christ died for us" (Romans 5:8). Nothing *forced* God to provide humanity with salvation from our justly deserved punishment. The very fact that God did not leave us to our own sinfulness—and with it the resulting pain and suffering—shows that He is a God of love.

If God is God, then everything that defines God must be equally present. God cannot be all love and just some righteousness. Rather, He has perfect love and is perfectly righteous. God provided a way to satisfy His justice *and* His love without violating our freedom. We will discuss this more in a later chapter. The fact God sent His Son to die on our behalf is what sets Him apart from any other deity in this world. The fact that the "Son of Man [came] to save that which was lost" (Matthew 18:11) proves beyond a shadow of doubt that God is love.

Did God Create Evil?

There are some who allege that God is the author of evil. The logic behind this accusation is this:

> God is the cause of all that exists.
> Evil exists.
> Therefore, God is the cause of evil.

The logic is impeccable, as far as the rules of logic go. If we deny the first point, we make God less than all He is. If we deny the second point, we fall into New Age or Eastern thinking. But as we learned earlier, God did not cause Adam's fall. So God is not the direct cause of evil. So where did evil come from? The answer is somewhat complex, so please bear with us.

The Different Kinds of Causes

When one says that God causes all things, he is correct in one respect, but such a general statement fails to distinguish the different types of causes. There are four ways in which God is causatively involved with the universe.

Because nothing would transpire in the universe if God had not created the universe, He is responsible, in one sense, for the evil that occurs. This is called *first cause*. The second type of cause is *formal cause*, in which God establishes the various rules by which the universe operates, issues of cause and effect, laws of nature, and the like. If human beings attempt to defy these laws, they will fail. God cannot be held responsible if, say, we try to fly off a mountain cliff. Third, there is *efficient cause*. This is the manner in which God works in the world to bring about His plans for all of creation. God chooses that He Himself will act or permit us to act in every situation of life. The fact that He allows us to act, and we do good or ill, does not make God the direct cause of the action. Only when God directly acts to alter a situation that would have happened otherwise is He the direct cause.

Last, there is *final cause*. This cause is the culmination of all the other causes. Because God chose, without necessity, to create a universe to operate within certain laws and He involves Himself in the world, actively or passively, this ensures that the final result of all things will bring about His perfect will and bring about the most good.

So did God cause evil? No, He certainly did not in the direct sense of efficient cause. Yet even though God allows humans to use their free will to commit sin, He will bring about ultimate good from human sinful actions through His sovereign will and infinite wisdom.

What Is Evil?

Evil is not a substance. In other words, evil does not exist on its own; it does not have self-existence. For example, you and I exist. We *are*. We have being, personality, self-awareness, and so on. In the same way, angels, demons, trees, birds, stars, oxygen, atoms, electricity, and so on *exist*.

Evil, however, is different. Evil can only exist within things that have being. For example, a human can be evil. A demon can be evil. And things that happen can be evil. Hurricane Katrina and the Holocaust were evil. But evil cannot *be* something. Bible scholar and philosopher Norm Geisler calls evil a parasite of being.[10] This does not deny that evil exists, but that it exists as its own being. The church theologian Augustine argued against the idea that there was some eternal Evil (in opposition to the eternal Good). He said that everything that God makes is good. We see this truth stated in Genesis 1.

Nothing God created is of itself evil. So that which is a creation of God is by nature good and not evil. But evil can *corrupt* creations. For example, humans were created without evil. Adam and Eve were by nature good. But their nature became evil by being corrupted. Augustine said that if you removed evil from created things, they would return to their natural good state. This is so with humans. Those who trust Christ will ultimately be returned to an uncorrupted state. The apostle Paul taught this in 1 Corinthians 15: "So when this corruptible has put on incorruption, and this mortal has put on immortality, then shall be brought to pass the saying that is written: 'Death is swallowed up in victory'" (verse 54). Indeed, every Christian should look forward to the day when evil will no longer be present in this world.

Augustine further restricted evil. He said that evil, rather than existing on its own, was a "loss of good." Augustine was criticized (accurately) for this definition. Not every absence of good is evil. The medieval theologian Thomas Aquinas helped solve this problem. He said that evil is a lack of some good that something *should have*. So a lack of sight is evil in a man, but not a rock. In the end, evil cannot exist without something *to corrupt*. So the logical argument given above fails because its second premise (evil exists) is wrongly understood.

God Did Not Create Evil

God does not create things without being. If evil is only the corruption of a good creation, a simple "loss of good" that something is supposed to have, then it is impossible for God to have created evil. To continue with the logical argument:

> God only creates things that have being.
> Evil does not have being.
> Therefore, God does not create evil.

God does not create a loss of something or a corruption. If evil cannot *be,* then God cannot be said to have made it *be.* Further, God does not create beings that are already corrupted or have no goodness, because God is incorrupt and good. This might sound like Spinoza, but there is an important difference. Spinoza said all things are *of* or *in* God. We, along with Augustine here, say things come *from* God. Whatever comes from God begins with the qualities of God. So then, God created a perfect world, and everything in it was perfect. But God alone is unable to be corrupted. We know that humans are not God, so it follows that we are not incorruptible. So when Adam and Eve sinned, their nature was corrupted, as was all of creation. And when all of creation was corrupted, evil was first present.

The Real Cause of Evil

If God did not create evil, then what caused evil? Theologians have said there is no *direct* cause of evil; rather there is an *indirect* one. This is because evil is defined as a lack of good, an absence of good. Something that is absent cannot have a direct cause (for reasons far too complicated to illustrate here). Consequently, the cause of evil is indirect—namely, freedom. Freedom is an indirect cause because the mere quality of freedom does not automatically produce evil. Geisler says, "Evil results when the free creature turns away from the infinite good of the Creator to the lesser goods of creatures. 'For it is evil to use amiss that which is good.' Freedom itself is a good thing, but evil results from a misdirection of this freedom."[11] He uses the example of Satan, the first being to become evil. Satan was not content to be under the rule of God; he wanted to be equal with God. In his freedom, he rebelled against God, an act that was evil.

As we will soon see, however, God is an *indirect* cause of evil.

Why Has God Allowed Evil?

We have seen that the presence of evil neither limits God's power nor knowledge, and does not mean He is unloving. And we have seen that God did not create evil. So then why does He allow evil? As we will discover, the fact God allows His creatures the freedom to sin ultimately will be used by Him to bring the greatest good.

TYPES OF EVIL

We must also keep in mind there are different kinds of evil. Generally we may classify two types: moral and physical (or natural). Moral evil is said to be that which humans perpetuate. We will discuss the evil of the Holocaust in World War II as an example of moral evil. Physical evil is described as those things in nature that are evil, such as Hurricane Katrina.

TYPES OF CAUSE

Building on our earlier discussion of the four types of causes, let us concentrate here on *direct* versus *indirect* cause. A *direct cause* is something that actively, intentionally causes something to happen. Genesis 1:1 presents a good example of a direct cause: "In the beginning God created the heavens and the earth." Here, God is the direct cause of the heavens and earth being created.

An *indirect cause* involves something that is somehow removed from the primary cause. Genesis 1:11-12 presents an example of this: God created vegetation with the capacity to reproduce. Genesis 1:12 describes for us the result of this capacity: "The earth brought forth grass, the herb that yields seed according to its kind, and the tree that yields fruit, whose seed is in itself according to its kind." The grass and herbs were the direct cause of the seeds, and God was the indirect cause. This is important to remember because we have said that God is the indirect cause of evil, not the direct.

GOD'S WILL, MAN'S FREEDOM

When God created the world and everything in it, He directly caused this creation, as we have seen, and did so by His will. However, He also created the conditions for things that were not His desire. In this way He indirectly caused them. Adam's moral freedom was directly caused by God. Adam was created this way. What Adam did with that freedom was not directly caused by God, but was an indirect result of God's decision to give humans moral freedom. As we learned earlier, it was a corruption of this freedom that caused evil.

In posing the issue of God's will and human freedom, one might ask, "Why didn't God create a world in which people had freedom but at the same time were unable to sin?" Or, "Could God have prevented Adam's sin?"

God created all humans with the capacity to act freely within their nature. Adam and Eve had the capacity to choose between obeying or disobeying God's command. We were created, as the Westminster Shorter Catechism says, "...to glorify God, and to enjoy him for ever."[12] Humans were not created as robots, nor were they created as merely possessing animal instincts. Animals do not recognize good or evil because they were not given the capacity to know these traits. A mistreated dog reacts in an instinctual way to physical pain, whereas humans who are mistreated somehow know such treatment is morally wrong.

Now, God had the power to stop Adam from sinning. He could have violated Adam's freedom by stepping in and preventing Adam and Eve from exercising free choice. This would have presented a problem, however. Humans are not programmed automatons who may be shut down and reprogrammed if a glitch develops. We are self-aware beings given an existence by our Creator. As such, God gave us the possibility of loving and obeying Him or hating and disobeying Him. This is the essence of human freedom.[13]

Along with this freedom came responsibility. God gave Adam the parameters of his freedom, and Adam violated those parameters. In doing so, he sinned. If God were to simply erase the consequences of our sin, we would not love Him for doing so because we would not know what sin and the absence of love are. God allows evil because He allows us freedom. We would not be free if there were no possibility of acting in an evil manner.

HUMAN SUFFERING CAN BE BENEFICIAL

We will see in later chapters that sometimes God allows or even directs things that, to us, seem evil. Sometimes pain and suffering are for our own good. Sometimes they are opportunities for us to show our character, faith, or patience. Sometimes the presence of evil gives rise to great good.

An example of this is the Holocaust, a very sensitive issue. It is argued by some people that God purposed that millions die in agony in order to establish the Jewish people in their homeland, Israel.[14] The argument follows that the Jews had endured great suffering for over 2000 years while living in exile in foreign lands. Yet there was no movement to establish the nation once again in the ancient homeland. Far more Jews were killed during these centuries than in World War II, let alone all those who suffered in other ways because of anti-Semitism. Something different happened in the Holocaust and served as a catalyst for good. This memory is burned into the mind and life of the Jewish people today. For example, military service is required of all Israeli citizens. Part of their training is touring various sites around Israel that are reminders of the great suffering that the Jewish people have endured.

When I (Wayne) take tour groups to Israel each year, I take them to a site known as Yad Vashem, a Holocaust memorial. This site leaves a tremendous impression upon the minds and hearts of tour members, who get a clear sense of the great suffering the Jewish people faced during World War II. The memorial's motto is "Never again." The Holocaust helped shock the world into finally taking steps to recognize Israel as a country. Until 1948, much of the world was indifferent to the idea of a Jewish state, but the horrors of the Holocaust finally persuaded the newly founded United Nations to act. Since 1948, Jews have had a homeland in which they can find some degree of peace and security.

Now, the good creation of the state of Israel does not negate the terrible evil the Nazis carried out during the Holocaust. It was human sin that led to the Holocaust, whether or not God used it for good.

On an almost infinitely smaller degree, I know of a young man who suffered a painful event which he believes was directed by God for his own good. This young man was very active and was, among many other things, a runner, a soccer player, and a downhill skier. He was so busy with life's pursuits that he gave little thought to God. Some of his friends had tried to point this out, but his attitude was one of rebellion against God. He had even said, "Don't bother; I don't need God."

This man was a proficient downhill skier. He would tackle the steepest slopes and ski off jumps as high as 20 feet tall. One winter he took a trip to Canada to ski. One beautiful morning, the sky was bright blue and six inches of snow had fallen the night before. It was 25 degrees, the perfect temperature for skiing. On his first run that fateful morning, he decided to warm up by skiing off the run and among the trees, which he had done many times before. As he was floating through the powder, he went off a little mound no more than three feet high. Just as he skied off the top of the mound, his left ski inexplicably rotated 90 degrees inward, and there was no time for him to correct it. He landed in a heap in the soft snow. Although he felt a little pain in his leg, he thought nothing of it until he tried to get going again. When he tried to move, his left knee popped out of its socket. It turned out he had ripped a ligament in his knee and needed surgery.

After the operation, the young man was confined to his living room floor with nothing to do but think. For the next six months he could not ski, play soccer, or run. He could not do any of the things that had been important to him. He became depressed, wondering why this would happen to him. As his friends told him more and more about God and His Son Jesus, the man came to realize he really did need God. He realized he was a sinner, estranged from God, and that he was bound for an eternity apart from God because of his sins. He also learned that Jesus had come to save him from his sins. Eventually he believed in Jesus as his Savior and went on to go to Bible college and seminary.

Looking back, he is convinced God caused the freak accident that sidelined him. There was no reason for his ski to do what it did, but he could clearly see the reason the accident happened. God used his pain and suffering to show him that he could not rely on himself and to break through his will. In this way the momentary suffering was nothing compared to what was gained, just as Paul said in Romans 8:18.

Man's Limited Understanding

As finite beings, we cannot possibly know or understand God's eternal knowledge. We see things from a very impaired perspective. How can we question what God is doing? The apostle Paul, in his letter to the Romans, anticipates those who would question God's decisions: "What shall we say then? Is there unrighteousness with God? Certainly not!" (9:14). Paul then quotes Exodus 33:19 and 9:16 and concludes, "Therefore He has mercy on whom He wills, and whom He wills He hardens" (9:18).

Anticipating the further argument that God is not fair because He acts in a way we think is arbitrary, Paul says, "But indeed, O man, who are you to reply against God? Will the thing formed say to him who formed it, 'Why have you made me like this?' Does not the potter have power over the clay, from the same lump to make one vessel for honor and another for dishonor?" (9:20-21). Paul then concludes with a glimpse of but one possibility as to why God does certain things:

> What if God, wanting to show His wrath and to make His power known, endured with much longsuffering the vessels of wrath prepared for destruction, and that He might make known the riches of His glory on the vessels of mercy, which He had prepared beforehand for glory, even us whom He called, not of the Jews only, but also of the Gentiles? (9:22-24).

Will God Ever End Evil?

We have seen that God is not the cause of evil, He is not powerless to stop it, and He is not callous to it. But will God ever do away with suffering? Most certainly! God has planned from eternity past to do so. He has revealed this plan through the apostle John. In the book of Revelation, we see the great culmination of this age and the glorious things to come.

In Revelation 20, God shows us how He will bring an end to evil. First, He will do away with the evil one himself: "The devil, who deceived them, was cast into the lake of fire and brimstone where the beast and the false prophet are. And they will be tormented day and night forever and ever" (20:10). When this is accomplished, God will deal with humanity. All the dead will be raised up and brought before the judgment seat of God. The Book of Life will be opened, and each person will be judged on whether their name is written in the book. John says, "Anyone not found written in the Book of Life was cast into the lake of fire" (20:15).

Those whose names are in the Book of Life will be given entrance into the eternal kingdom of God, and will enjoy His presence forever. In light of this wonderful promise, we should take heart and be courageous in the face of evil.

Chapter Four

Why Does God Allow Pain in Our Lives?

If you were God, what kind of world would you have created? Would it be free of suffering? Would all people treat each other with dignity, love, understanding, and justice? Would you have created people who have the freedom to act consistent with their full potential?

These are interesting questions, and we wonder why God didn't make things this way. But the fact is, He did. When God created the world, it had all these features. It is *humanity* who brought all the troubles we know in the world, through willful transgression of the law of God. Yet in spite of this, because of God's great love toward His creation, He made available a plan of redemption that will bring harmony to the world once again for all eternity.

We know from the preceding chapter that God has allowed physical and moral evil in the world. He has allowed humans free will to fulfill an ultimate purpose that He has designed for the universe, and for us in particular. It is hard to accept the difficulties and sufferings of life, but the person of faith continues to trust God in the midst of pain and in spite of it. We who are Christians are followers of Jesus, who for the joy that was set before Him endured the cross (Hebrews 12:2). We are like those heroes of old who accepted even torture and death at the hands of sinful men "that they might obtain a better resurrection" (Hebrews 11:35).

In the last chapter we focused on the problem of evil itself. Now we would like to address why evil comes our way, and why God allows evil to happen. We might think that we would respond to evil differently, and deal with it immediately. But we have to guard against such thinking for at least two reasons. One, God is perfect, and we're not. We do not have the wisdom and foresight He has. And two, if God had dealt with sin immediately, all of us would have been condemned to eternity without Him because we are sinners worthy of judgment. Rather, God is loving and longsuffering, giving adequate opportunity for rebellious, sinful people to believe in Him unto salvation. God *will* deal with sin and evil and will be victorious, but that will happen in His timing, and not ours.

Will Even the Faithful Experience Pain?

If pain is a curse, and Christians are forgiven, then why do Christians still experience pain? Aren't Christians lying down in green pastures and being led by still waters (Psalm 23:2)? Are these metaphors not inconsistent with pain?

When I (Wayne) was a boy, an evangelist came to our small new church for a revival meeting. His name was Harrison E. Price. I remember his rugged features and deep gravelly voice as he sang what was apparently one of his favorite songs, "It's Not a Bed of Roses." The words of the chorus of that song have stayed with me even after several decades: "Oh, it's not a bed of roses, you will have to take the bitter with the sweet, you will have your tests and trials and temptations every day, no it's not a bed of roses all the way."[1]

I don't know if anyone remembers or sings that song anymore but it stuck in my mind. Both bitter and sweet come into our lives. We should anticipate that struggles will come, and we must learn why they come, how to avoid them if possible, and how to trust in God in the midst of them. Will even a dedicated servant of God experience emotional or physical pain? This may be answered in the affirmative both from Scripture and contemporary events.

One of the most well-known passages of Scripture is Hebrews

chapter 11. Here are described a number of heroes of the faith. Similar to a baseball or football hall of fame, Hebrews chapter 11 is a biblical hall of fame. When we "walk" the corridors of this hall, we notice patriarchs, kings, warriors, and prophets. They founded nations and kingdoms, fought great wars, and proclaimed the very words of God. This is all very exciting. But further along in the chapter, we see another set of faithful heroes. Instead of being victors, they appear to have been vanquished. Note the contrast, but don't miss the conclusion:

> Others were tortured, not accepting deliverance, that they might obtain a better resurrection. Still others had trial of mockings and scourgings, yes, and of chains and imprisonment. They were stoned, they were sawn in two, were tempted, were slain with the sword. They wandered about in sheepskins and goatskins, being destitute, afflicted, tormented—of whom the world was not worthy. They wandered in deserts and mountains, in dens and caves of the earth.
>
> And all these, having obtained a good testimony through faith, did not receive the promise, God having provided something better for us, that they should not be made perfect apart from us (Hebrews 11:35-40).

Did you notice the end? All the heroes—and us—are destined for perfection or final maturity not based on what the world considers to be success but on what God seeks: faithfulness. God has great plans for each of us so that through victories and seeming defeats we might reach the goal He has for us: "My brethren, count it all joy when you fall into various trials, knowing that the testing of your faith produces patience. But let patience have its perfect work, that you may be perfect and complete, lacking nothing" (James 1:2-4).

The apostle Paul recognized the struggles that would come his way because of his ministry in the gospel (Acts 20:17-23), but then he offered an inspiring statement of victory: "None of these things move me; nor do I count my life dear to myself, so that I may finish my race with joy, and the ministry which I received from the Lord Jesus, to testify to the gospel of the grace of God" (Acts 20:24).

About 35 years ago, an old church bus from a Southern California town rambled down a dark highway in Mexico. In the bus were 30 or so high-school students from a large Baptist church. Their destination was a mission church at which they would do ministry work. The driver was the youth pastor; he was quite a guy! He often grinned in the joy of the Lord, "Jehovah Jireh [the Lord will provide], brother, Jehovah Jireh." He wore a crew cut and looked every bit like a Marine drill sergeant. He had a fiercely powerful handshake to complement his appearance.

No one could possibly doubt this youth pastor's dedication to our Savior, his dutiful work in ministry to God, or his devotion to his family. He was quite devoted and successful as a husband and a father. In fact, his daughter, whom I will call Marcia, was on the bus making the same trip.

After the youth pastor had spent long, tiring hours behind the wheel, the bus somehow ended up veering off the highway. It turned on its side and flipped over. The youth pastor was knocked unconscious. When he awoke, he was immediately filled with concern for his young charges. He asked the Mexican official if the kids on the bus were okay. The reply was that all but one was just shaken up. The one exception was a girl who had been thrown through one of the bus windows, and then the bus had rolled over her, crushing her to death. "Who was that?" the youth minister asked. His heart was wretched with crushing pain upon being told it was his own precious daughter, Marcia. He, and others, cried out, "Why, God?"

As this example indicates, even dedicated people of God have pain. The fact that God's people experience pain is clearly taught in Scripture: "For your sake we are killed all day long" (Romans 8:36). Even Joseph, whom God was very pleased with, was sold into slavery (Genesis 37) and upright Job lost his sons and daughters by tragedy (Job 1).

How Should We Respond to Pain?

Knowing that we are sure to experience suffering, this naturally leads us to the following question: How should we respond to pain?

A young woman in Holland was known for her concern for children with disabilities. She was so energetic in her work that she also founded young girls' clubs during the 1920s and 1930s. Her desire was to be like her father, a watch repairman in Haarlem, and she became the first female watchmaker licensed in the Netherlands. She had an older sister, Elizabeth (Betsie), who was born with anemia, and a brother who was a theology school graduate who wrote a thesis on anti-Semitism.

Everything was going well for the ten Booms until the Nazi invasion of Holland in 1940. After this invasion, Corrie ten Boom's girls' clubs were banned. The ten Boom family began to secretly harbor Jews in a hiding place in their home until they were discovered on February 28, 1944. The entire family was arrested. The father died a few days after his arrest. Corrie and Betsie were sent to the infamous Ravensbrück concentration camp in Germany, where they ministered comfort and the Bible to fellow prisoners. While there, Corrie's beloved sister Betsie died. Before she did, however, she said memorable words to Corrie that provided strength to her during the remainder of her internment: "There is no pit so deep that God's love is not deeper still."

Corrie was released, by a clerical error, from the concentration camp on Christmas Day in 1944, just a week before the Germans killed the other women prisoners of her age.[2]

Corrie ten Boom (b. 1892) died in 1983, less than a decade after I (Wayne) had the privilege of being with her for a brief time. I will never forget her cheerful and loving spirit. In her talks she would tell the audience that life looks like a multicolored and mangled group of threads on the back of a tapestry. The threads seem unrelated and make no sense; all appears to be purposeless and confused. Yet when the tapestry is turned around, we see beautiful woven colors with intricate detail, and a clear sense of design by the weaver.

So it is with all of life. Pain, disappointment, persecution, rejection, death, and other tragedies may seem so meaningless and hopeless, maybe leaving us in despair. But here on this sin-filled earth, we are looking at the back side of the tapestry. Were we to look at life from the weaver's perspective, we would understand that it all makes perfect sense. "There is no pit so deep that God's love is not deeper still."

Is God Really in Control?

So how are we to respond to pain? Corrie's sister put her confidence in the love of God. The youth pastor who lost his daughter continued to trust in the love, grace, and power of God. This is practical theology! We should remember and be convinced that God is with us and is watching out for us. Rather than let pain exercise control over our faith, we should keep pain under faith's control.

Where does such unshakeable conviction in God come from? How can we continue to trust Him when tragedy hurts us so greatly? The answer is found in the conviction that our God is in charge. God controls events; events do not control God!

As the psalmist affirms,

> He only is my rock and my salvation, my stronghold; I shall not be greatly shaken...On God my salvation and my glory rest; the rock of my strength, my refuge is in God. Trust in Him at all times, O people; pour out your heart before Him; God is a refuge for us. Selah.
>
> Men of low degree are only vanity, and men of rank are a lie; in the balances they go up; they are together lighter than breath. Do not trust in oppression, and do not vainly hope in robbery; if riches increase, do not set your heart upon them.
>
> Once God has spoken; twice I have heard this: That power belongs to God; and lovingkindness is Yours, O Lord, for You recompense a man according to his work (Psalm 62:2,7-12 NASB).

You can trust God at all times because "power belongs to God"! This is what we need to remember in our times of greatest difficulty, when we wonder if God is really in charge. Though this world is on a frenzied roller coaster ride jarring and turning and rising and falling, God is not just another passenger on the roller coaster. Though our lives may seem to be bouncing freely out of control, we must keep in mind we see things from a limited earthly perspective. God has a plan in all this that should give us optimism even when we suffer. This divine plan means that all things, even tragic things, that happen to us are under the sovereign, divine dominion of an almighty God who loves us dearly. God has power; He is in charge!

Is God's Plan Based Just on God's Foreknowledge?

When it comes to God's plans for our lives, we may wonder: Is God's plan just a result of God knowing ahead of time what men and women will do, or is God's foreknowledge a result of His plan? How we answer this will depend on whether we view our experiences as influencing God, or we believe God has a plan from eternity past into which we fit. If the latter is true, then God is in control of His world. And if the former is true, then God is a reactionary being who makes plans based on what we do. Key to all this is a proper understanding of the Greek terms translated "foreknew" and "foreknowledge" in the Bible.

The word "foreknew" in Romans 8:29 is a translation of the Greek verb *proginosko*, which, rather than referring to things about which God has information, refers to a relationship with individuals that God Himself begins. So the word means more than just God knowing something ahead of time.[3] The same verb is used in Romans 11:2—there, it speaks of God's *choosing* the nation of Israel, and not a *mere knowledge* of what Israel will do.[4]

This word is also found in 1 Peter 1:2 as a noun (Greek, *prognosis*) and once more again in the New Testament in Acts 2:23. In Acts 2:23, Peter was not saying just that God knew something would happen before it happened—that is omniscience. Peter coupled "foreknowledge" with the phrase "the determined purpose" of God. That speaks of a plan set in advance. So, divine foreknowledge, which refers to more than just an awareness of the future, means that God works His will in His creation, establishing boundaries for His plan.

For example, we see God's plan at work in the decisions made by Joseph's brothers in Genesis 45:5-8, Cyrus in Isaiah 44:28, and those responsible for the death of Christ in Acts 4:27-28. These specific examples support the general and universal principle that God is in control, just as Isaiah 46:10 and Ephesians 1:11 say He is. So, should we presume that foreknowledge simply means that God knows in advance what will happen (which He does), and then adjusts His plan accordingly (which He does not need to)? Such a view cannot explain the evidence, which strongly suggests we should hold to the understanding that God *knows* the future because God has *planned* the future. The truth that God is in control and sovereign over all things is affirmed by the psalmist: "Our God is in heaven; He does whatever He pleases" (Psalm 115:3).

God does what He pleases!

Does God Control All Events or Just Some?

Yet another good question in relation to our suffering in this: Does God control all things, or just some? The way in which we answer this question affects how we will deal with suffering. Were it true that God controls only some things, then of course there might be reason to doubt whether our pain is part of God's plan or not.

But there seem to be no events excluded from God's control. "All things" are accomplished "according to the counsel of His will," not just some (Ephesians 1:11). God supplies *all* our needs, not just some of them (Philippians 4:19). God upholds *all* things, not just some (Hebrews 1:3). "*Whatever* the LORD pleases He does in heaven and in earth, in the seas and in all deep places" (Psalm 135:6, emphasis added). God exercises His control over *all* that happens. Some theologians, like those who espouse Open Theism, deny that God has settled all things from eternity.[5]

Now, if we affirm that God does control all things, does that mean that He *directly causes* all things?

Does God Exercise Both Prescriptive and Permissive Control?

Is saying that God controls all things the same as saying He is the direct and only cause of all things that happen? Or does God use other causes, such as nature and man's will? Scripture indicates that God causes some things, and other things He simply allows to happen. Both sorts of events are included in God's all-comprehensive plan.

Knowing this helps to answer another issue connected to God's sovereignty. If God controls all things, how can human will be free? Cannot pain be the exclusive result of bad choices that we make with complete and unqualified freedom, untouched by any divine plan?

That humans make their own decisions is clear in Scripture. Yet at the same time, God made decisions in eternity past, solely based on His sovereign will and perfect wisdom, either to act or to refrain from acting at every instance within time and space. Usually God permits people to make decisions regarding how they will act, but He sometimes intervenes, as with Balaam in Numbers 22–23, or the prophet Jonah, when human action would countermand divine purposes. At times God may choose to act in judgment because of human sin and rebellion (for example, His judgments against Egypt through the ten plagues) while at other times allowing humans to exercise their own choices that nonetheless fulfill His judgment (for example, Assyria's war against Israel in the seventh century B.C.). Other examples include God's punishment of Ananias and Sapphira for lying (Acts 5:1-11), and God permitting a man to be born blind and remain that way until Jesus healed him so that God could be glorified (John 9).

Even in reference to sin, we see in the Bible that God is involved indirectly. For example, God *permits* some things to happen that He does not directly cause. God may, for example, allow sin: "In past generations he allowed all the nations to walk in their own ways" (Acts 14:16 ESV). But *permitting* sin is not *causing* sin, for God does not make anyone sin (James 1:13). God allows, in His permissive will (an indirect cause), the wills of evil persons (Exodus 7:3-4) or even the will of Satan (Job 1:12; 2 Corinthians 12:7) to affect us. In any case, whether God uses indirect causes or not, "a man's steps are directed by the LORD" (Proverbs 20:24 NIV). God does whatever He pleases both in heaven and on earth (Daniel 4:35). Just as God plans, so it happens (Isaiah 14:24)!

Does God promise painlessness and prosperity? This does not appear to be the case in Scripture. Although we do see examples in which, after a time of suffering, God will bring blessings. After Joseph was sold into slavery and spent time in prison, God made Joseph powerful and rich (Genesis 41:42-43). And after Job lost everything he had, "the LORD blessed the latter days of Job more than his beginning" (Job 42:12). Job ended up with 14,000 sheep, 1000 yoke of oxen, and 6000 camels! And he was given seven sons and three daughters. A wealth of possessions and family were given Job after God removed his pain.

On the basis of these examples, should we believe that God always desires to give prosperity and health to His people? Should we expect the pain to be followed by a great blessing of wealth and health and the end of our suffering? Those who promote what is called the Prosperity Gospel, argue yes, for the following reasons:

1. They say Christ died so that we would have money. "Though He was rich, yet for your sakes He became poor, that you through His poverty might become rich" (2 Corinthians 8:9). It was not wealth, however, that Christ gave up. In this passage, "rich" relates not to money and luxury, but to relationship to God (Philippians 2:6-8).

2. They say Christ died so we would have health. "By His stripes we are healed" (Isaiah 53:5). But this blessing of physical healing is not wholly ours until that future time when our bodies are redeemed: "The sufferings of this present time are not worthy to be compared with the

glory that is to be revealed in us...we ourselves groan within ourselves, eagerly waiting for the adoption, the redemption of our body...this corruptible must put on incorruption, and this mortal must put on immortality" (Romans 8:18,23; 1 Corinthians 15:53). We all know that our bodies are decaying, not getting better. We also know that many who claim this Prosperity Gospel doctrine of health immediately consult with physicians when they, or their loved ones, become gravely ill, unlike what they advocate for their followers. Too many examples of this exist to deny it.

3. They say if God's people do not have money, then God is robbed of pleasure. "The Lord...has pleasure in the prosperity of His servant" (Psalm 35:27). Here, the word "prosperity" is the Hebrew term *shalom,* which usually does not mean being wealthy, but being in peace.

4. They say the reason some Christians are not rich is that they do not have the faith to believe that God wants to make them prosperous. "According to your faith let it be to you" (Matthew 9:29).[6] But there is no place in the Bible where Christians are told to pray for wealth. In fact, Jesus told us to lay up our treasures in heaven, not on earth (Matthew 6:19-21).

In contrast to such teaching is Peter's statement, "Let those who suffer according to the will of God commit their souls to Him in doing good" (1 Peter 4:19). Nothing says our pain will be brief, or that pain immediately precedes prosperity and perfect health. Rather, Peter says that pain may be God's will.

Why Does God Allow Pain in Our Lives?

Our Pains Lead to Denial of Our Sufficiency

There is a general view in society—and even among many Christians—that all of life is meant to be happy and absent of problems, struggles, and pain. When someone goes through a serious sickness or is injured, particularly if young, we view this as somehow inconsistent with how life ought to be. Life is to be trouble free, or so we may think.

But as we've already seen, Scripture says we will experience suffering. Here are a couple reasons this is the case:

Our Spiritual Deprivation Builds Character and Dependence upon God

It is not through easy times that character is built. And it is not in times of happiness that our true character is revealed to others. It is when we are tried by suffering that we grow in perseverance, patience, and trust. It is pain that leads us to turn to God for help. As a result, we grow spiritually stronger and draw closer to God.

Our Suffering Reminds Us We're Not Home Yet

The Bible says we are strangers and pilgrims in this world (2 Corinthians 5:1,5; Hebrews 13:14; 1 Peter 2:11). The pains and difficulties of this earthly existence are a stinging reminder to us that this world is not our permanent home. It is in times of suffering that the saying, "This world is not my home; I am just passing through" takes on new meaning.

What Are the Sources of Our Suffering?

We discussed this briefly earlier but now will turn our attention to a more in-depth look at the reasons why we suffer.

Trouble Comes from Others

Some people find themselves trapped in circumstances not of their own doing. For example, they may have been born into a home of extreme poverty, drug abuse, or physical abuse from a mother or father. Or a person may grow up under tyrannical political regimes that bring different types of hardships and abuses, often including persecution for belief in Christ. None of these situations are the fault of the person experiencing the suffering but because of the existence of sin within fallen humanity, he is the recipient of pain. The Bible promises there is coming a future time of judgment in which justice will prevail for those who suffered wrongly.

We Bring Our Own Trouble

Others suffer pain in their lives as a result of their own sinful activities. Someone who refuses to work may bring poverty on himself as well as those around him. The mother who has a fixation on a live-in boyfriend may allow him to beat her and her children. A person may bring distress upon himself because he is lazy. It is not uncommon, as the writings of Dalrymple have aptly shown,[7] for a person to wallow in misery due to laziness and be coddled by a society that accepts corporate guilt. Laziness can be accompanied by immorality, dodging of accountability, and a rebellion against one's moral training and against God.

Some people love things and use people instead of loving people and using things. They cheat and lie to get ahead. In doing so, they can bring negative consequences upon themselves. For example, those who gamble may lose their entire livelihood and that of their family. By whatever manner, much of our misery is brought on by sinful acts.

Troubles Come as the Discipline of God

Yet another source of pain is the chastisement or the testing of God. God disciplines His children when they disobey—not to bring some kind of pleasure to Himself, but to bring repentance and a change of life. God knows that our continued involvement in sin brings serious repercussions. Thus He brings judgment for our spiritual well-being. God stressed the benefits of obedience and warned against disobedience in Deuteronomy 30:19-20:

> I call heaven and earth as witnesses today against you, that
> I have set before you life and death, blessing and cursing;
> therefore choose life, that both you and your descendants
> may live; that you may love the LORD your God, that you

may obey His voice, and that you may cling to Him, for
He is your life and the length of your days; and that you
may dwell in the land which the LORD swore to your
fathers, to Abraham, Isaac, and Jacob, to give them.

Similarly, the apostle Paul said that the judgment he proposed for
the believer who was involved with his father's wife was ultimately for
his eternal benefit:

It is actually reported that there is sexual immorality among you, and such sexual immorality as is not
even named among the Gentiles—that a man has his
father's wife! And you are puffed up, and have not rather
mourned, that he who has done this deed might be taken
away from among you. For I indeed, as absent in body
but present in spirit, have already judged (as though I
were present) him who has so done this deed. In the
name of our Lord Jesus Christ, when you are gathered
together, along with my spirit, with the power of our
Lord Jesus Christ, deliver such a one to Satan for the
destruction of the flesh, that his spirit may be saved in
the day of the Lord Jesus (1 Corinthians 5:1-5).

Those who are unresponsive to God's discipline may be judged
even with the loss of their life. This becomes plain in the case of many
of the Israelites (1 Corinthians 10:1-22), and New Testament believers
as well. Ananias and Sapphira are prime examples (Acts 5:1-11), and
warnings along this line appear in James 5:20 and 1 John 5:16-17. The
eternal consequences may be found in 1 Corinthians 3:9-15, where it
is revealed by Paul that a person, based on his works in this life, may
be saved but lose all of his heavenly rewards. In spite of the severity of
some of the discipline dispensed by the Lord, Scripture tells us that
it is remedial, not retributive, in nature. God chastises us to save us
from worse, or to bring us back to a life that is healthy and reflective
of His image:

You have forgotten the exhortation which speaks to you as to sons: "My son, do not despise the chastening of the LORD, nor be discouraged when you are rebuked by Him; for whom the LORD loves He chastens, and scourges every son whom He receives."

If you endure chastening, God deals with you as with sons; for what son is there whom a father does not chasten? But if you are without chastening, of which all have become partakers, then you are illegitimate and not sons. Furthermore, we have had human fathers who corrected us, and we paid them respect. Shall we not much more readily be in subjection to the Father of spirits and live? For they indeed for a few days chastened us as seemed best to them, but He for our profit, that we may be partakers of His holiness. Now no chastening seems to be joyful for the present, but painful; nevertheless, afterward it yields the peaceable fruit of righteousness to those who have been trained by it (Hebrews 12:5-11).

What Are the Benefits of Our Suffering?

The apostle Peter comforts us with this affirmation that our suffering brings us to greater spiritual maturity:

In this you greatly rejoice, though now for a little while, if need be, you have been grieved by various trials, that the genuineness of your faith, being much more precious than gold that perishes, though it is tested by fire, may be found to praise, honor, and glory at the revelation of Jesus Christ, whom having not seen you love. Though now you do not see Him, yet believing, you rejoice with joy inexpressible and full of glory, receiving the end of your faith—the salvation of your souls (1 Peter 1:6-9).

Indeed, the crucible of suffering refines and strengthens us.

Our Troubles Bring Glory to God

In our suffering, it is very possible for us to serve God and bring glory to Him. We see this in John 9, where John recounts the story of a man born blind. Several things are amazing about this account. First, the apostle has taken a whole chapter—a little over five percent of the entire book—to talk about an anonymous blind man. Clearly, the healing of this man has special importance to John's presentation of Jesus. Second, the people immediately concluded that the man's blindness was the result of personal sin (either his own, or that of his parents). They assumed that the righteous are healthy and in favor with God, and the sick (and probably poor) are unrighteous and lack God's favor (9:2). This same type of conclusion has been preached by today's proponents of the Prosperity Gospel.

Third, this man's blindness occurred at or before birth, so surely he had not committed any personal act of sin that brought this malady on him (9:1,20). Fourth, when Jesus performed the healing, He demanded faith that required action on the blind man's part. He had to wash in the pool of Siloam (9:7). Fifth, Jesus proclaimed that the man had been blind in order that the "works of God" might be displayed through him (9:3). This indicates that some sickness and suffering that we endure could very well promote the purposes of God. And finally, though the man was physically blind, the greater blindness was the spiritual kind shown by the Pharisees (9:39-41). This spiritual blindness is worse than physical pain, suffering, and trials, for it condemns people to eternity apart from God.

Ultimately, the blind man had a calling. God allowed his blindness so that others might see the works of God and glorify Him. The same can happen today when a saint of God endures pain, and even death, that encourages sinners toward repentance.

I (William) know of a man named Jack. He taught at a local junior high school. He was a large, powerful man who also coached the wrestling team. He was always smiling, very much enjoying the love and grace of God. Eventually Jack was diagnosed with lung cancer. As the days went by, the people at his school could observe his waning and weakening. He lost strength, energy, size, and hair, but he kept coming to work. Finally, Jack required assistance to walk, and day after day his wife drove him to school. Upon arriving at school, his wife supported him on one side and his daughter supported him on the other. They would help him down the hall to his classroom and to his chair. From there, Jack would teach.

What did all this pain and difficulty accomplish? Much! Others could see by Jack's faith that God had not abandoned him. Others could see strength in weakness and grace in pain. Never was a more powerful sermon preached on the power of God than Jack walking down the school's hall with the help of his loved ones. Each difficult step was a psalm to God's glory; each day of Jack's life was a new chapter of God's grace. Jack's uncompromised compliance with and acceptance of God's plan for his life edified all those around him.

Jack's lack of complaints about God's will and his determination to serve despite ever-increasing weakness were profoundly visual illustrations of what the apostle Paul stated in Philippians 4:11-13:

> I have learned to be content in whatever circumstances I am. I know how to get along with humble means, and I know how to live in prosperity; in any and every circumstance I have learned the secret of being filled and going hungry, both of having abundance and suffering need. I can do all things through Him who strengthens me (NASB).

No scholarly interpreter of Scripture and no golden-tongued preacher can make it plainer than did Jack in his silent suffering that we, even in severe pain, even facing death so near, may bring glory to our God.

Why might our pain be good? One answer is that pain may be our ministry. It may be our calling. It may be our occasion, our opportunity, and even more, our obligation to serve and glorify our God. Both the Christians and non-Christians on that junior high school's faculty and in that student body witnessed the Savior's glory

and power because of Jack's quiet faith in God despite his severe
suffering.

One great example of how God uses our suffering is the apostle
Paul. Consider the ways he experienced pain, as described in 2 Corinthians 11:23-27.

> In imprisonments? Yes!
> In beatings? Yes, times without number.
> In feeling the lash? Yes, five times, with
>   thirty-nine lashes each time.
> In stonings? Yes, three times.
> In many dangers? Yes.
> In shipwrecks? Yes, three times.
> In hunger and thirst? Yes.
> In cold and exposure? Yes.

Why did Paul suffer so much? God said that pain was to be part of
Paul's ministry: "He is a chosen instrument of Mine, to bear My name
before the Gentiles and kings and the sons of Israel; for I will show him
how much he must suffer for My name's sake" (Acts 9:15-16).

Years ago, Campus Crusade used to hand out a booklet that said,
"God has a wonderful plan for your life." I suspect that many who
read the booklet believed that to accept Jesus would bring a life free
of discomfort, sickness, and difficulties. What if the booklet had said,
"Accept Jesus, and you will suffer much for His name's sake"? How
many would have been attracted to the gospel? Yet this is the calling
of the Christian—not a life of ease, but of service and even pain.

Paul knew why he suffered. He wrote, "If we are afflicted, it is
for your comfort and salvation" (2 Corinthians 1:6). Through Paul's
suffering, others were served. Suffering can be both providential and
purposeful. And we can trust our God to remain ever faithful in our
pain resulting from tribulation, distress, persecution, famine, naked-
ness, peril, and even death (Romans 8:35-39).

Our Troubles Keep Us Humble

In 2 Corinthians 12:7 Paul wrote, "To keep me from exalting myself, there was given me a thorn in the flesh, a messenger of Satan to torment me—to keep me from exalting myself!" (NASB). Evidently Paul needed to experience some sort of pain to offset his significant experience of God's revelatory grace. Various suggestions have been offered as to what the "thorn in the flesh" was. Murray J. Harris summarized these: "Jewish persecution, carnal temptation, epilepsy, chronic opthalmia, a speech impediment, and a recurring malady (such as malaria or Malta fever)."[8]

Regardless of what Paul's infirmity was and whether it was physical or mental, Paul indicates both its purpose and his reaction to it. At first Paul repeatedly asked God to remove his suffering. God's reply was that in Paul's weakness, His power would be perfected! Paul, therefore, preferring pain with God's power to painlessness without God's power, affirms that he is "content with weaknesses...for Christ's sake; for when I am weak, then I am strong" (verse 10 NASB). In pain, therefore, we may become perfected. Our suffering may bring us to experience God's strength. Paul was better off with his thorn in the flesh than without it!

God "disciplines us for our good, that we may share His holiness" (Hebrews 12:10 NASB). We should remember that those who bear fruit for God are enabled to be even more productive when they let God cut the dead wood away from the vine (John 15:2). This divine act might cause us pain.

Can Pain Help Us Understand God's Grace and Mercy?

One of the most tragic stories in the Old Testament is that of the child who died after David arranged to make Bathsheba a widow (2 Samuel 11:1-17), then took Bathsheba as his wife (verse 27). The child's death was a divine punishment (verses 15-23).

What did David learn from this? Psalm 51 tells us. David cast himself on God's great grace and mercy and confessed, "I was brought forth in iniquity" (verse 5). He asked for cleansing: "Wash me, and I shall be whiter than snow" (verse 7). He asked for restoration: "Create in me a clean heart, O God...Restore to me the joy of Your salvation" (verses 10,12). We should note that David, in making these requests, anticipated God's mercy. David's painful repentance led him to God's grace!

Twenty-five hundred years later, a young German experienced similar spiritual anguish. He suffered because he had a great fear of a malevolent deity. He had a deep conviction of his own unworthiness, saying of himself that he was but dust and ashes and full of sin. He tried to ease his guilt by doing good works. He fasted days at a time without a crumb. In his room in the cold cloister, he would throw off the blanket that provided the very minimum of warmth available and would allow himself to freeze, heaping more suffering upon himself. He also prescribed for himself vigils and prayers far beyond that required of his own order. As his biographer explains, Martin Luther probed every resource of his Roman Catholic faith in attempts to relieve the anguish of a spirit alienated from God.[9]

Finally, in 1515–1516 while lecturing on Romans and Galatians, Luther found God's grace. He developed a new view of God: God the terrible is also God the merciful. Divine wrath and divine love fuse on the cross. For Luther, suffering led to a realization of the mercy and grace of God.

We today can learn from Luther. Only humility realizes God's greatness. Only repentance receives God's forgiveness. And only weakness obtains God's strength.

Suffering Helps Us Understand the Suffering of Others

Through our suffering, we come to better understand the suffering others endure. And we can especially come to appreciate those who suffer for God and His Word.

In many parts of the world, Bibles are plentiful and inexpensive. They are readily available in different translations, and we can buy leather-bound ones or ones with Christ's words in red or ones with ample explanatory notes written by scholars. Publishers compete with each other to sell Bibles, and Christians must have the newest and best. Churches supply Bibles in pews, and the Gideons and others make Bibles available in hotels and in other ways. But such plenitude has not always been the case.

There was a time, before the printing press was invented, when the preciousness of Scripture meant not only that its content was exceedingly valuable but also meant that copies of it were rare. Scripture was laboriously copied by hand, so it took a long time to produce even just one Bible. To be a keeper of a copy of the Scripture in the fourth century A.D., as was Timothy, a deacon of Mauretania (an ancient province of Rome in present-day Morocco and Algiers), was a high and responsible calling. As it turned out for Timothy, it was also a very dangerous calling.

At the beginning of the fourth century, the Christian church had experienced 40 years of relative repose from persecution by the Roman Empire. That was to change. With the ascent of the emperor Diocletian, Christians were persecuted even more vigorously than before, and this lasted from A.D. 303–311. The edicts of Diocletian included the destruction of all Christian churches. Christians who were unwilling to offer sacrifices to the Roman gods were to be martyred. Most relative to Timothy's story, Diocletian demanded that all Bibles were to be burned.[10]

Roman soldiers under direction of Governor Arrianus came to Timothy and demanded that he turn over God's Word for burning. Timothy's wife, Maura, pleaded with her husband to agree to the governor's demand, but Timothy refused. He said that he would sooner give up his own children than God's revelation. So Timothy was hung upside down, dangling from his feet, with weights around his neck and a gag in his mouth. Finding even this to no avail, the soldiers proceeded to heat red-hot irons with which to put out Timothy's eyes.

Maura was greatly anguished by the torment Timothy endured, and this caused her to realize the reason for her husband's suffering. This was not punishment from God. This was not consequent to a sin Timothy had committed. Her husband's suffering was on account of his commitment to God!

When we see someone suffering, let us not ask, as did the disciples, "Who sinned, this man or his parents?" (see John 9:2). Suffering and difficulty are not always punishment from God. They do not necessarily indicate the person is out of God's will. Pain is to be expected even by the faithful when they take a stand for God. And this should bond us together in Christ.

Not only did Maura come to understand and even appreciate the cause of her husband's suffering, she committed herself to join Timothy in his pain. She stopped begging her husband to relent and also became resolute in refusing to yield up the Scripture to the governor's fire. Consequently, Maura and Timothy were crucified together in A.D. 304. Together, they suffered to bring glory to God.[11]

Jesus Has Identified with Us in Our Suffering

Let us now turn to Jesus and His sufferings, a topic that we will investigate in more detail in chapter 7. For now, we are only concerned with the question of whether pain served a benefit for Christ. Did pain perfect Christ? Scripture says, "He Himself was tempted in that which He has suffered" (Hebrews 2:18), and "Although He was a Son, He learned obedience from the things which He suffered. And, having been made perfect..." (5:8-9 NASB).

The sufferings of Christ evidently had a positive effect on Jesus Himself. He learned from them, and was perfected. But how can God, who *already* is all-knowing and changeless (Psalm 102:26-27; 137:5; Malachi 3:6; Hebrews 1:10-12; 13:8), learn obedience and be perfected?

For the answer, we need a clear understanding of Christ's person. And a good place to begin is Philippians 2:6-8:

> Who, being in very nature God, did not consider equality with God something to be grasped, but made himself nothing, taking the very nature of a servant, being made in human likeness. And being found in appearance as a man, he humbled himself and became obedient to death—even death on a cross!

Here are several observations about these verses: First, Christ exists in two natures — God and man. Second, Christ is only one person, as the pronoun "he" and the verbs are singular, despite the fact He has two natures. The person works through each nature in the manner appropriate to that nature. Referring to the matter of Jesus suffering, Gregory of Nyssa wrote that Christ's divinity did not suffer or die because that would constitute a change in God; God is changeless.[12]

These observations are consistent with the view that Christ, in addition to being true God, is also true man. The humanity of Jesus clearly is a scriptural doctrine:

1. Christ is said to be a man (John 4:29; 7:46; 11:47; Acts 2:22; Romans 5:57; 1 Timothy 2:5).
2. Christ underwent experiences common to humanity (Matthew 4:2; John 4:6; 12:27; Hebrews 4:15).
3. Christ developed as does a man (Luke 2:40; Hebrews 5:8).
4. Christ has the essential human physical and psychological faculties of a man (Luke 2:52; 22:42; John 12:27; 13:21; Hebrews 2:14-17).

It follows, given that Christ is both God (who cannot be perfected) and man (who can be perfected) that the sufferings of Christ, which resulted in His learning obedience and His being perfected, occurred in the humanity of Christ, not in His deity.

But we must at once dismiss the notion that the perfecting of Christ in His humanity, which likely included resisting temptation (Hebrews 4:15),[13] had anything to do with moral improvement. The morality of Christ cannot be improved because He always did the will of His Father (John 8:29). Christ is ever without sin (John 8:46; 2 Corinthians 5:21; Hebrews 4:15; 1 Peter 2:22). So it seems that what Christ meant by being perfected is that the trials and temptations He endured through perfect obedience served as preparation for His redemption of us by His death. As Paul said, Jesus was obedient even to the point of death on a cross (Philippians 2:8).

Certainly the passion was the principal occasion for Christ to suffer. And that included physical anguish. But before the cross, our Lord endured many other things: temptation, rejection even by His own people and some family members, ridicule, homelessness, weariness, and persecution. We have no evidence that He was ever ill, but we do know that He expected to die (Luke 9:22), and this expectation may have weighed heavily on His mind even in His earlier ministry, as it did when the passion week began. Luke describes for us the emotional pain of Jesus in Gethsemane: "Being in agony, He prayed more earnestly. Then His sweat became like great drops of blood falling down to the ground" (22:44). This is our Lord experiencing terrible mental suffering.

Is Christ's Suffering an Example to Follow in Our Suffering?

While our pain cannot be seen as being redemptive for others in the exact sense as is Christ's pain, the Bible indicates that we should consider the sufferings of Christ to be an example for us in enduring our pain. Thus Peter writes, "You have been called for this purpose, since Christ also suffered for you, leaving you an example for you to follow in His steps" (1 Peter 2:21 NASB). We are, therefore, *called to suffer!*

Far from encouraging us to avoid all pain, Peter affirms that "to the degree that you share the sufferings of Christ, keep on rejoicing" (1 Peter 4:13 NASB). We are to rejoice when we suffer in God's will! The idea of suffering with Christ is expressed in Luke 9:23 as well. There, after saying that "the Son of Man must suffer many things," (verse 22 NASB), our Lord challenges us to pick up our own crosses, which we suppose includes our suffering daily. To take up our cross may be to suffer in God's will. Perhaps this is Paul's meaning when he says, "I have been crucified with Christ," (Galatians 2:20), and "I die daily" (1 Corinthians 15:31).

It should be noted that Scripture differentiates between just and unjust suffering. While Peter endorses enduring unjust suffering as a testimony to God, regarding just suffering the apostle wrote, "Let none of you suffer as a murderer, a thief, an evildoer, or as a busybody" (1 Peter 4:15).

In this chapter we have seen that pain may be God's will for us, and we have seen the potential good effects of our suffering. Let us not shrink back from what God has brought to us, but embrace the acts of God in faith so that we might glorify Him by whatever He chooses to do in our lives.

Part Two:

Getting to Know the God Who Feels Our Pain

Chapter Five

Getting to Know the God Who Cares for You

You can never *love* a person more than you *know* that person. And you can rarely come to know a person more than that person is willing to be known. And we can easily claim to love someone, but true love demands sacrifice. To develop a relationship with another person, to discover the real person, requires time and effort. This is true about getting to know God.

Now, God has done His part. He made a profound sacrifice to demonstrate His love (John 3:16), and He has known us intimately and exhaustively—forever (Romans 8:28; Ephesians 1:4). That's what we know about God's love for us. But what about our love for God?

It is not uncommon for Christians to speak of loving God. Yet many have not taken time to study Scripture carefully to find out about the God who has made Himself known to us in His Word. Often we merely superimpose onto God our ideas of who He should be based on our personal preferences. When confronted with certain truths about God as found in Scripture, some people say, "That is not the God I worship," and that may be true. After all, many of the ancient Israelites served a God who does not exist. The only God who is real is the God who reveals Himself in the Bible.

Paul the apostle said, "Even if there are so-called gods, whether in heaven or on earth (as there are many gods and many lords), yet for us there is one God, the Father, of whom are all things, and we for Him; and one Lord Jesus Christ, through whom are all things, and through whom we live" (1 Corinthians 8:5-6). The Israelites had hardly left Egypt when they began to worship God in a manner opposite of His commandments (Exodus 32:4), and even in the Promised Land they worshipped idols under the name of God (Judges 17:3). We, too, can use the term *God* and yet be envisioning a being who is different from the true God. In C.S. Lewis's classic book the *Screwtape Letters,* Uncle Wormwood challenged his demon nephew Screwtape to maneuver his human assignments to begin to create a mental image of God that would lead them to worship the god of their imagination rather than the true God.

Why is it important for us to come to a better knowledge of the attributes of God in relation to whether He truly "feels" for us in life's struggles? The reason is that expecting God to think or act in ways that conform to our desires may leave us with frustration or even anger at God when we are asking Him to be something other than He is, or to do something other than how He acts. God is not a butler whom we summon to serve our desires, a policeman to call only when we are in trouble, a doting grandfather who satisfies his grandchildren's every whim, or a Santa Claus who brings gifts based on whether we are naughty or nice.

Some decades ago A.W. Tozer wrote a wonderful little book entitled *The Knowledge of the Holy.* In it, Tozer speaks to the importance of knowing who God is:

> A right conception of God is basic not only to systematic theology but to practical Christian living as well. It is to worship what the foundation is to the temple; where it is inadequate or out of plumb the whole structure must sooner or later collapse. I believe there is scarcely an error in doctrine or a failure in applying Christian ethics that cannot be traced finally to imperfect and ignoble thoughts about God.

It is my opinion that the Christian conception of God current in these middle years of the twentieth century is so decadent as to be utterly beneath the dignity of the Most High God and actually to constitute for professed believers something amounting to a moral calamity.[1]

When we think of God, we must not view Him in human terms (Numbers 23:19). We must not expect Him to act as we would act, particularly because so many of our attitudes and acts would be beneath Him. God's acts of mercy and grace do not come from moods that He experiences, but instead are based on His perfect, infinite, and harmonious attributes. He is not sometimes one way and sometimes another. He is eternally all of what He is in perfect wholeness.

None of God's attributes are inactive at any time, nor are they ever in conflict. For example, God's love is not in conflict with His justice, His righteousness with His mercy, or His knowledge and wisdom with His decrees. This is important to understand because God's concerns for us are not whimsical or temporary, but purposeful, genuine, and eternal. Knowing this truth can help us gain comfort.

Apologist Norm Geisler provides several reasons we should gain a proper understanding of God. First, all of our Bible doctrine (theological truth) depends on understanding God's attributes. For example, if God is not holy, then there is no standard against which to contrast our sinfulness and our need for salvation. If God is not just, then there is no need to deal with man's sin and avoidance of hell by the death of Jesus Christ on the cross.

Second, the Bible often tells us to avoid false teachers and false prophets. We would not know who they are unless we know who the genuine God is.

Third, ideas have consequences. Beliefs are important because they lead to action. It was the belief systems of Hitler, Stalin, Mao Tse-Tung, and other evildoers that led to the slaughter of millions of innocent lives. As tragic as these are, false belief in God can lead to negative eternal ramifications.

Fourth, our spiritual growth is directly affected by our concept of God. A person tends to become like those whom he admires. When we look to the image of Jesus, we can be transformed into His image (2 Corinthians 3:18). Our spiritual growth is directly affected by our efforts to know God better. Tozer rightly said in the first sentence of his excellent book, "What comes into our minds when we think about God is the most important thing about us."[2]

Fifth, and last, we will never be truly satisfied in life unless we find our satisfaction in God. Augustine said, "Thou awakest us to delight in Thy praise; for Thou madest us for Thyself, and our heart is restless, until it repose in Thee."[3] And the psalmist David said similarly, "As the deer pants for the water brooks, so pants my soul for You, O God" (Psalm 42:1).

It is beyond the scope of this chapter to develop a comprehensive statement of who we know God is according to His revelation. We will, however, identify Him to the extent that we are able to avoid following after some other god of our imagination and miss the true God when He does meet us in our need, and trust Him even when He does act in ways different from what we desire.

The Uniqueness of God

Orthodox Christians have united for many centuries around the uniqueness of God's being. Brian Davies lists these elements of God's uniqueness under the unusual classification of "the oddness of God." I would prefer to use the term *unique,* but the idea is the same: God is unlike everything else.

1. God is the source of the existence of absolutely everything other than Himself.
2. God is not an item in the universe.
3. God acts in or on what is not divine not as something external but as a source of existence.
4. God is not something in nature of which can be distinguished from the individual that it is.

5. God's nature is to exist (or, God exists by nature).

6. God does not undergo (and cannot undergo) any real change.[4]

God is wholly other than His creation, and the ways in which His creation, including humans, is like God only approximates what God is like. Because of God's absolute uniqueness, we can know that (1) God is incomparable, (2) God is incomprehensible, and (3) God must be spoken of in metaphorical terms when compared with His creation.

The Incomparable God

HOW INCOMPARABILITY IS EXPRESSED IN THE BIBLE

The living God, Yahweh, shared certain characteristics in common with the gods of the nations that surrounded Israel, but these false deities cannot properly be compared to Him.

Let us illustrate what we mean: One may say that an ant is similar to a human being. The similarities are that ant and human both exist, have form, are living creatures, occupy space and time, have bodily parts, and a few other points of comparison. But because the gap between the two is so very great, we can say that an ant cannot be truly compared to a human being.

Using this as an illustration is inadequate as we attempt to explain the correspondence between humans and God, because God is intangible, unlimited, and exists totally outside of our experience, whereas humans are tangible, limited, and knowable by nonsupernatural means. Thus we learn by comparing what *is known* to what *is unknown,* but with God we cannot learn of Him apart from direct revelation that He has given us in nature and in Scripture. The biblical text says of God, "My thoughts are not your thoughts, neither are your ways my ways, declares the LORD. For as the heavens are higher than the earth, so are my ways higher than your ways and my thoughts than your thoughts" (Isaiah 55:8-9 ESV). Consequently, everything that we say of God may be said only because He has chosen to give us this particular information about Himself.

In 1996, C.J. Labuschagne came out with a book, possibly the first of its kind, in which he set forth the theology of the Old Testament about the incomparability of Yahweh.[5] His research reveals there are three primary ways in which God's incomparability is stated in the Old Testament. First is the *negative expression,* such as "There is none like..."[6] as in the following examples:

> No one is holy like the LORD, for there is none besides You, nor is there any rock like our God (1 Samuel 2:2).

> At this time I will send all My plagues to your very heart, and on your servants and on your people, that you may know that there is none like Me in all the earth (Exodus 9:14).

> Among the gods there is none like You, O Lord; nor are there any works like Your works (Psalm 86:8).

> Inasmuch as there is none like You, O LORD (You are great, and Your name is great in might), who would not fear You, O King of the nations? For this is Your rightful due. For among all the wise men of the nations, and in all their kingdoms, there is none like You (Jeremiah 10:6-7).[7]

These passages emphasize that God has no competitors among the alleged gods of the nations.

The second manner in which God's uniqueness is declared carries the same meaning as the negation above and is stated by a *rhetorical question,* such as "Who is like...?"[8]

> Behold, he shall come up like a lion from the floodplain of the Jordan against the dwelling place of the strong; but I will suddenly make him run away from her. And who is a chosen man that I may appoint over her? For who is like Me? Who will arraign Me? And who is that shepherd who will withstand Me? (Jeremiah 49:19).

Who is like me? Let him proclaim it. Let him declare and set it before me, since I appointed an ancient people. Let them declare what is to come, and what will happen (Isaiah 44:7 ESV).

Who is like the LORD our God, who dwells on high...? (Psalm 113:5).

Who is like You, O LORD, among the gods? Who is like You, glorious in holiness, fearful in praises, doing wonders? (Exodus 15:11).

Who is a God like You, pardoning iniquity and passing over the transgression of the remnant of His heritage? He does not retain His anger forever, because He delights in mercy (Micah 7:18).[9]

Only two of the above passages declare God's incomparability, but all of them indicate that God cannot properly be compared to other gods in regard to His character and His deeds for His people Israel.

A third manner of expression is that of using *verbs that denote equality and similarity*.[10] For example:

Who in the heavens can be compared to the LORD? Who among the sons of the mighty can be likened to the LORD? (Psalm 89:6).

Many, O LORD my God, are Your wonderful works which You have done; and Your thoughts toward us cannot be recounted to You in order; if I would declare and speak of them, they are more than can be numbered (Psalm 40:5).

"To whom then will you liken Me, or to whom shall I be equal?" says the Holy One (Isaiah 40:25).

Nothing and no one can be on the same level as Yahweh, the Creator and Sovereign. These three ways of speaking about Yahweh reveal that He is not viewed as comparable with other gods or with anything else in all His creation. All of the imitations of deity and the machinations of men that are set against this true God demonstrate their impotency.

The New Testament also advances the teaching that God is incomparable. One way it does this is by the use of the words "only" or "alone" for God:[11]

> Jesus said to him, "Away with you, Satan! For it is written, 'You shall worship the LORD your God, and Him only you shall serve'" (Matthew 4:10).

> Jesus answered and said to him, "Get behind Me, Satan! For it is written, 'You shall worship the LORD your God, and Him only you shall serve'" (Luke 4:8).

> How can you believe, who receive honor from one another, and do not seek the honor that comes from the only God? (John 5:44).

> This is eternal life, that they may know You, the only true God, and Jesus Christ whom You have sent (John 17:3).

> Of that day and hour no one knows, not even the angels of heaven, but My Father only (Matthew 24:36).

> Why does this Man speak blasphemies like this? Who can forgive sins but God alone? (Mark 2:7).

> The scribes and the Pharisees began to reason, saying, "Who is this who speaks blasphemies? Who can forgive sins but God alone?" (Luke 5:21).

The uniqueness of God's existence gives rise to the incomparable nature of His being. Only God is to be worshipped. Only God can give eternal life. Only God has knowledge of the future and can forgive sins.

In the New Testament, another manner in which God is shown to be incomparable is by the *use of doxologies*. These splendid exclamations are like shouts of praise to the indescribable, incomparable deity whom we worship. Paul often broke out into spontaneous praise (Romans 11:36; 16:27; Galatians 1:5; Ephesians 3:21; Philippians 4:20; 2 Timothy 4:18), and the half-brother of Jesus, Jude, wrote one of the most complete doxologies. Here are a few such praises to God:

> Now to the King eternal, immortal, invisible, to God who alone is wise, be honor and glory forever and ever. Amen (1 Timothy 1:17).

> ...which He will manifest in His own time, He who is the blessed and only Potentate, the King of kings and Lord of lords, who alone has immortality, dwelling in unapproachable light, whom no man has seen or can see, to whom be honor and everlasting power. Amen (1 Timothy 6:15-16).

> Now to Him who is able to keep you from stumbling, and to present you faultless before the presence of His glory with exceeding joy, to God our Savior, who alone is wise, be glory and majesty, dominion and power, both now and forever. Amen (Jude 24-25).

Profuse praise of God is often found in the writings of the fathers of the early church. Here are two examples that capture the manner in which God is to be adored. First is a statement from Theophilus, who uses negative predications to describe the being of God:

> The appearance of God is *ineffable* and *indescribable* and cannot be seen by eyes of flesh. In glory God is *incomprehensible*, in greatness *unfathomable*, in height *inconceivable*, in power *incomparable*, in wisdom *unrivaled*, in goodness *inimitable* in kindness *unutterable*.[12]

Next is an example from the extrabiblical Gospel of Peter, in which the author uses both negative and positive predications of God:

Recognize now that there is one God...the *Invisible* who *sees* all things; the *Incomprehensible* who *comprehends* all things; the One who needs *nothing,* of whom all things stand *in need,* the *Uncreated,* who *made* all things by the word of his power.[13]

HOW GOD'S CHARACTER AND ACTIONS DECLARE HIS INCOMPARABILITY

We also see God's incomparableness through His character and His actions. We first observe that *He is incomparable because He is the Creator:*

> Who has measured the waters in the hollow of His hand, measured heaven with a span and calculated the dust of the earth in a measure? Weighed the mountains in scales and the hills in a balance?...
>
> It is He who sits above the circle of the earth, and its inhabitants are like grasshoppers, who stretches out the heavens like a curtain, and spreads them out like a tent to dwell in...
>
> Lift up your eyes on high, and see who has created these things, who brings out their host by number; He calls them all by name, by the greatness of His might and the strength of His power; not one is missing (Isaiah 40:12,22,26).

This is similar to the words that God spoke to Job in rebuke of Job's pride in believing that he could answer back to God for the sicknesses and misfortunes he had experienced.

> Then the LORD answered Job out of the whirlwind, and said: "Who is this who darkens counsel by words without knowledge? Now prepare yourself like a man; I will question you, and you shall answer Me. Where were you when I laid the foundations of the earth? Tell Me, if you have understanding. Who determined its measurements? Surely you know!" (Job 38:1-5).

God is the Creator, and we humans are the creatures. This is obvious, but we often forget our place in this world and begin, like Job, to believe that we may legitimately put the sovereign Creator on the witness stand to find Him somehow guilty for our difficulties. This is presumptuous and arrogant on our part, and it is part of our sinful propensity. If we wait on the Lord, we will find that God is merciful and will come to our aid (Job 42:12-17).

Second, *God's incomparability is confirmed by His transcendence.* He is above and apart from His creation, which we will discuss more a bit later. Suffice it to say at this point that He is outside of creation and thus cannot truly be equated or compared to it.

Third, *God is superior and unlike the gods of the nations* around Israel: "To whom then will you liken God? Or what likeness will you compare to Him? The workman molds an image, the goldsmith overspreads it with gold, and the silversmith casts silver chains" (Isaiah 40:18-19). In Isaiah 44:10-19, God mocks false worship in which people create a god that can provide no benefit, a god that is not the living God. Man will cut down a tree, use some of the tree for warmth and baking food, and with the remainder, he creates a god to worship and cries out "Deliver me, for you are my god!" (verse 17). Such foolishness was not limited to the ancient Israelites.

A few days after the destruction of the World Trade Center in New York City on September 11, 2001, I (Wayne) was on a plane to Korea. I talked with a woman who sat in the same row I was in. She commented that in such difficult times, it was important that we have something to believe in, to hold onto. I agreed, and asked, "Whom should we believe in?" She said it was not important whom or what we believed in as long as we believed in *something.* I responded with another question: "What if I believed in Buddhism, Hinduism, or the gods of other religions besides Christianity? Would that make any difference? She said no. I then asked, "Is it okay for me to believe in the Easter Bunny or the Tooth Fairy simply because they make me feel good?"

My point was similar to what God said in Isaiah 44: Why believe and worship a god who is not alive, is not real? What benefit does one receive in believing and worshipping a nonexistent god?

Fourth, *all nations of the world are not comparable to God.* They are as nothing. One of my favorite films, released in 1982, *Chariots of Fire,* tells the story of two athletes at the 1924 Olympic games—Eric Liddell and Harold Abrahams, runners from Scotland and England. The movie won multiple Oscars and was nominated for others. Two of the most moving portions of the movie relate to Eric Liddell. When Liddell found out that he would need to compete on Sunday, what he viewed as the Sabbath, he refused to run because he considered doing so as contrary to God's law.

In refusing to run Eric had to stand against the Olympic committee and the Prince of Wales, the next king of England. The prince told Eric that everyone at times must show loyalty to their nation by sacrificing other commitments to which they hold. Liddell responded by saying that it is God who sets up kingdoms and brings them down, and that he would not surrender his commitment to obeying the law of God.

On the Sunday Eric was to have run the 100-meter race, Eric Liddell was standing behind a pulpit delivering a sermon. He quoted from Isaiah 40, describing the nations as nothing before the Creator:

> Have you not known? Have you not heard? The everlasting God, the LORD, the Creator of the ends of the earth, neither faints nor is weary. His understanding is unsearchable (Isaiah 40:28).

> All nations before Him are as nothing, and they are counted by Him less than nothing and worthless (Isaiah 40:17).

The achievements of men and governments are small in comparison to the creative acts of God.

Finally, *God is independent of His creation* and has no need to be content or for anyone or anything to exist. Only as He has chosen to involve Himself in His creation, including us, does He have need. Isaiah poses questions that accentuate this truth:

> Who has directed the Spirit of the LORD, or as His coun-
> selor has taught Him? With whom did He take counsel,
> and who instructed Him, and taught Him in the path of
> justice? Who taught Him knowledge, and showed Him
> the way of understanding? (Isaiah 40:13-14).

Isaiah tells us that God is self-sufficient and independent of humans and does not need us to give Him guidance (see more on this in chapter 9). No one has been God's counselor or teacher. No one needs to tell the all-knowing and all-good God what is just or right. No one measures up to God's nature or standards.

When we say that nothing can be compared to God, or that God is incomprehensible, we seek to preserve the uniqueness of God and separate Him from His creation. This is very important in our religious climate today because Eastern and New Age religions believe that God is part of His universe and should be understood as the same as the world. Such thinking is foreign to the Bible.

The Incomprehensible God

To say that God is *incomprehensible* is to say He is far more than we can speak or imagine. It is not only little children who ask, "What is God like?" This question challenges us all through life.

When we speak of the incomprehensibility of God, we are not saying God is without attributes or is absolutely unknowable. This is what liberal theologian Paul Tillich taught. He said the true God is not knowable. To Tillich, for one to describe God is to lose the true God. This is not what we are suggesting. When we say God is incomprehensible, we only mean that God is so far above His creation and human experience that unless He chooses to reveal Himself, we can know nothing about Him. And even with God revealing Himself, there is always an element of mystery about Him. An infinite deity cannot be known completely by a finite human. So we must distinguish what

God is like in Himself, then, from what has God disclosed about Himself.

Nicholas of Cusa stated the idea of incomprehensibility in these ways:

> The intellect knoweth that it is ignorant of Thee because it knoweth Thou canst not be known, unless the unknowable could be known, and the invisible beheld, and the inaccessible attained.[14]

> If anyone should set forth any concept by which Thou canst be conceived I know that that concept is not a concept of Thee, for every concept is ended in the wall of Paradise...So too, if any were to tell of the understanding of Thee, wishing to supply a means whereby Thou mightest be understood, this man is yet far from Thee... forasmuch as Thou art absolute above all the concepts which any man can frame.[15]

How May We Speak of God?

As we attempt to plumb the depths of the indescribable God, we naturally encounter the difficulty of how to speak about Him. Often when people speak about God, they wrongly attribute to Him characteristics that do not truly reflect the divine being. To be biblical, we must distinguish that-which-is-God from that-which-is-not-God, to use A.W. Tozer's words. In order to do this properly, we need to understand the different ways one might speak of God and whether these are appropriate. We may speak of God's attributes in three different ways—namely, equivocally, univocally, or analogically (see Figure 1).

Equivocally

To speak of God equivocally is to use the attributes of God in totally different ways than they are understood in reference to finite beings. We speak equivocally when we employ a term in a unique sense so that it is completely different in another context. For example, consider how the word *row* is used in these phrases: "a row of trees," and "row the boat." The word *row* appears in both phrases, but its meaning changes. Were we to speak of God in equivocal terms, we would know nothing about God, for He would be entirely different from anything true of creation, and would be totally apart from our own experience. Because all our knowledge moves from the known to the unknown, we would have no words with which to speak about God because there would be nothing we could compare Him to. This perspective of God may lead to skepticism.

Univocally

Univocal descriptions are used when speaking of the attributes of God and those of finite creatures in entirely the same ways. A term employed in a univocal sense is used with different subjects but has the same sense in their contexts with these subjects. For example, in the phrases "the man is tall" and "the building is tall," the word *tall* means the same thing in both. Were we to speak of God in univocal ways, whatever we say about finite creatures would be true of God in the exact same way. Yet it's not possible to compare an infinite being with finite beings.

Equivocal	Univocal	Analogical
Term employed in only one sense, so a term has completely different meanings in a context from its other meanings	Term employed predictively with different subjects has the same meaning in both instances	Combination of equivocal and univocal
A row of trees and row the boat	The man is tall and the building is tall	Jeff runs the 100 yard dash, and the train runs down the track

Figure 1: How We Speak of God

Analogically

To speak analogically is to combine the univocal and equivocal ways of speaking, such that the attributes of God and finite creatures are applied similarly. For example, were we to say, "Jeff *runs* the race on the *track*" and "The train *runs* on the *track*," the terms *run* and *track* carry similar meaning to each other but are not identical. This is the manner of speaking of God when we recognize that the creation represents a similarity to God but always falls short of His infinite and perfect nature. No other method of speaking of God's attributes fits the teaching of Scripture and experience. That we must speak of God analogically is very important as we consider the question of whether God "feels" our pain. Does God or can God even have feelings that include empathy and suffering?

Literal truth is sometimes expressed by the use of analogical language. So when Scripture says that God's eyes roam throughout the earth, the truth conveyed is the pervasiveness of God's presence, but the use of "eyes" is a metaphor, because God is not a physical being with eyes. The metaphor accentuates the literal truth of God's omnipresence.

When Scripture says that God does not remember our sins any longer, the literal truth expressed is that God no longer holds our sins against us, not that He has divine Alzheimer's disease. The metaphor is anthropopathic (human passions)—it is a human way to express a great divine truth.

Remember, humans were created in the image of God, so we are *theomorphic*—that is, after the form of God. He has created us with abilities or attributes that approximate in part what He is apart from finitude and from human form. God sees and we see, but we do so with the physical organs while God sees in infinity without physical eyes. We think and God thinks, but we do so in a limited manner and sequentially, while God thinks infinitely and intuitively with all knowledge being instantly before Him.

We have emotions and receive them as part of being made in God's image, but His emotions are not fickle, or opposed to reason.

Moreover, His emotions are completely consistent with His entire being for all eternity. When we are in pain, then, God's concern for us is not stirred at an instant in time; rather, He has been concerned from all eternity!

We must be careful with analogies because they may cause us to think of God in ways that are ignoble of God. For example, many of the analogies suggested regarding the Trinity end up teaching heretical views about God, leaning toward tritheism or modalism. Some analogies, however, are permissible, and if the figures are not extended too far, teach truth about God because they are divinely revealed in Holy Scripture.

Even those who wrote the Scriptures had difficulty here. Tozer says,

> The effort of inspired men to express the ineffable has placed a great strain upon both thought and language in the Holy Scriptures. These being often a revelation of a world *above* nature, and the minds for which they were written being a *part* of nature, the writers are compelled to use a great many "like" words to make themselves understood.[16]

We must, then, speak of God as He has revealed Himself to us rather than creating a God that conforms to our own personal preferences. And we are helped in our understanding of God in the most complete way by the incarnation of Jesus the Messiah. As we have said, God is unlike His creation and above it; unless He reveals Himself, He cannot be known. And that is the whole point of God entering into human history, revealing Himself in the Bible and most intimately through the Lord Jesus Christ. When we have seen Christ, we have seen the unseen God (John 1:18), our heavenly Father (14:9).

GOD IS ABOVE HIS CREATION

Pagan religions of the Mediterranean and ancient near-Eastern world identified God with nature. Thus the finite nature of the world carried over to their belief in finite gods. Whether it be the Greek Zeus or the Mesopotamian Marduk or the Canaanite Baal, these gods were controlled by the elements of nature; they did not control nature. The ancients failed, and even modern New Age religion fail, to see God before and over the created order. Moreover, in debasing God, they elevated humans. This is particularly true with Eastern religions and New Ageism, in which humans can become God. The Bible, however, does not permit us to make this bold step. Though humans are created in the image of God, and we are blessed with something unique and better than the rest of creation, still, we are only human.

One of the unique features of Israelite religion, in contrast with the pagan religions of the nations that surrounded Israel, was the belief that God was not a nature God. Rather, the God of Israel stood above nature, or creation, controlling it with His power and using it for His purposes. This is one of the special features of the first chapter of Genesis.

The first verse of the Bible contains far more pivotal information for the theology of the Bible than many of us may realize: "In the beginning God created the heavens and the earth" (Genesis 1:1). In those few words, several basic theological truths about God are discovered.

First, the passage sets forth the priority of God to the universe, something that Semitic cultures could not envision. Modern man has difficulty with this as well. The biblical text assumes the existence of God as a first truth from which all other existence arises. Second, one immediately recognizes that matter is subsequent and subservient to personality. That is, God is first and foremost. Third, God created the universe *ex nihilo,* out of nothing, not out of Himself or out of matter. Before time and space, only God existed. Thus, the first verse of the Bible starts out with a "big bang" in that it is a rejection of atheism (no God), polytheism (many gods), fatalism (chance), pantheism (identification of God and the world), materialism (all is matter), and naturalistic evolution (the universe came into existence spontaneously and moves from chaos to cosmos). It also denies the eternal nature of matter and affirms the eternal nature of God. As well, the transcendental nature of God is affirmed—He is above His world, not within it.

All these facts serve to remind us we must not attempt to bring the Creator God down to our level or force Him to measure up to our expectations, because to do so is idolatry.

The theme in Genesis 1:1—the fact that the true and infinite God is before and above the finite universe—is continued in the remainder of the first chapter of Genesis. Unlike the accounts of creation found in the pagan cultures around Israel, the God of the Hebrews does not emerge out of nature, but creates the world. Instead of fighting with other deities, as found in nature religions, God molds the inanimate forces of the sea, the moon, and the sun. With ease He creates, and all nature complies with His command.

When the Infinite God Reaches Down

A few years ago, during a flight across America, I (Wayne) was sitting at a window on the plane and looking at the scenery far below. As I was contemplating, I thought of how helpless I was on that plane. News reports of recent plane crashes flashed through my mind. I thought, *If something should go wrong with the engine or there were a terrorist attack, there would be nothing I could do to prevent the tragedy.* Driving a car and having control of the wheel is one thing, but 30,000 feet in the air is another, and provides little security. I took some solace in the presumed competency of the airline pilots, but even they were not in ultimate control.

Then it dawned on me that I and everyone else are dependent on God, because all of us are flying through the Milky Way galaxy in the vastness of space. Were a large asteroid to come toward earth, there is nowhere to hide, nowhere to escape. I began to appreciate afresh the faithfulness of our God to care for us, putting humans on a small planet in a small solar system with all the protections we have to preserve us. He has taken tender care of His special creation. Among all the trillions of heavenly bodies, the Bible portrays God as especially interested in us, with even the sun, moon, and stars provided for our benefit (Genesis 1:14-18).

Once we embrace the fact of our creatureliness and our need to depend on God, we may glory in the greatness of God as did the psalmist in Psalm 113. The greatness of Yahweh must be mentioned because it serves as a rationale for why His people are to praise Him. One of the psalms calls on the servants of God to praise Him because He is exalted above the heavens:

> Praise the LORD! Praise, O servants of the LORD, praise the name of the LORD! Blessed be the name of the LORD from this time forth and forevermore! From the rising of the sun to its going down the LORD's name is to be praised. The LORD is high above all nations, His glory above the heavens. Who is like the LORD our God, who dwells on high, who humbles Himself to behold the things that are in the heavens and in the earth? He raises the poor out of the dust, and lifts the needy out of the ash heap, that He may seat him with princes—with the princes of His people. He grants the barren woman a home, like a joyful mother of children. Praise the LORD! (Psalm 113:1-9).

All peoples throughout the earth rightfully praise Yahweh, the God of Israel, for all time according to verses 1-3. Then the psalm proclaims the sovereign transcendence of the Lord: He is high above the heavens, and cannot be properly compared to anything in creation (verses 4-5). He is so great above the universe that it is necessary for God to humble Himself just to look at the things within the universe (verse 6). As spectacular as this description of God is, for the purposes of this book, verses 7-9 are the most important part of this description. The Lord doesn't only bow down to the heavens and the earth, but also comes near to His creatures to rescue them so that He might exalt them and care for them.

Note that the God who is above the heavens reaches into rubbish heaps of life to rescue His people. The Hebrew word for "ash heap" (*asûpoœt*) refers to more than just dirt; it speaks more of the garbage in which pigs wallow. We may look at ourselves as pristine, but in reality we are far less. Our righteousness, the prophet Isaiah said, is like soiled garments: "We are all like an unclean thing, and all our righteousnesses are like filthy rags; we all fade as a leaf, and our iniquities, like the wind, have taken us away" (Isaiah 64:6).

What is so wonderful is that in spite of our wretched condition, God desires to render aid. In the book of Zechariah, the character of the redeeming God is revealed: "He answered and spake unto those that stood before him, saying, Take away the filthy garments from him. And unto him he said, Behold, I have caused thine iniquity to pass from thee, and I will clothe thee with change of raiment" (Zechariah 3:4 KJV). As stated in Psalm 113:7, here we see Yahweh, who is clothed in majesty and glory, come down into the mud and filth with us to get us out.

And not only does the Lord rescue us, He then puts us in the palace alongside royalty (Psalm 113:8). As Paul said in Ephesians 1:3-5, God chose us for Himself before the creation of the universe, and in Christ He has raised us to heavenly places.

The last verse in Psalm 113 carries special significance in the Semitic culture. To be without children was considered a great curse. Children were very important to the Hebrew home. They provided the continuation of the family, helped in providing a livelihood, and also took care of the parents in their old age. Not to have children would make life lonesome and difficult. Yet the Lord gives the barren woman a home and a house full of children. As my Bible-teacher friend Ronald B. Allen has said, "Diapers all around." This kind of inexpressible joy is what God desires for His children.

GOD CARES FOR US

The depiction of God as revealed in Psalm 113 is seen elsewhere in the Old and New Testaments. One Old Testament passage that demonstrates the care and love that God has for His people is this:

Now it happened in the process of time that the king of
Egypt died. Then the children of Israel groaned because
of the bondage, and they cried out; and their cry came
up to God because of the bondage. So God heard their
groaning, and God remembered His covenant with
Abraham, with Isaac, and with Jacob. And God looked
upon the children of Israel, and God acknowledged them
(Exodus 2:23-25).

The text here has four distinct words that describe the suffering of
the Hebrews under Egyptian bondage—"groaned," "cried out," "cry,"
and "groaning." When Moses wrote that Israel groaned because of the
bondage, he used a Hebrew word that means "to sigh or groan." This
word tended to be used to speak of the act of mourning in public, like
wailing and weeping at a funeral.[17]

The second phrase, "cried out," comes from a Hebrew word with the
root meaning "to cry for help in time of distress" and with a "disturbed
heart," needing help.[18] The third word means "a cry for help"—and is
from a Hebrew verb expressing intensity. It is used "to describe the cry
of anguish, the cry of the oppressed, the cry of those who are approach-
ing the breaking point."[19] The last Hebrew term carries the meaning,
"the groaning of oppressed people; of a wounded man."[20]

One may see from the multiple use of words describing despair
and suffering that Moses was attempting to bring empathy upon the
conditions from which the sons of Israel could not remove themselves.
They were moaning audibly, crying from their hearts in distress, in
anguish so great that they were at the breaking point. Who would
look kindly on them? Certainly not their captors, who punished and
oppressed them. Certainly not other Israelites, who were in equally
dire straits. Their cry came before the only one who could help them,
the God of their fathers.

Moses indicates that the Lord was faithful to the covenant that
He had made with Abraham, Isaac, and Jacob. His heart was deeply
touched by His people's plight. It is not readily apparent, but God

responded with concern to their distress call in four different ways. The text indicates that He "heard," "remembered," "looked," and "acknowledged" the Israelites.

Hebrew scholars Brown, Driver, and Briggs say that the Hebrew word for "heard," as found in Exodus 2:24, usually speaks of hearing that comes with the favor of God when God is the subject.[21] We discover that God hears with purpose, and words from His servants do not fall idly from their mouths. He is eager to assist.

Next, Exodus 2:24 says that Yahweh remembered His covenant with the patriarchs. The covenant provides the basis of God's actions, to fulfill His act of love begun with Abraham and now continued through Abraham's posterity. Though the text does say that God "remembered," we should not understand that to mean somehow God had truly forgotten His people. The use of "remember" is merely Moses speaking in a human manner (anthropathic) about God. The Hebrew term here tells us that God gave special attention[22] to what He had promised to the fathers. Then we read that God "looked" on the plight of the children of Israel.[23] From this observation comes the last of the four words describing God's concern, possibly the most powerful in the passage. MacDonald and Farstad write "God was not oblivious to the plight of His people. When a new king ascended to the throne, God heard and remembered and looked upon the children of Israel and acknowledged their condition."[24] But something more than mere acknowledgement of His people is involved in this passage. Moses speaks of God's knowledge of the Israelites, using a Hebrew word for "know" that does not merely refer to cognitive knowledge of someone or something, but expresses "intensive involvement" that "exceeds a simple cognitive relationship in the sense of 'to be concerned with.'"[25] The text clearly indicates that God had great empathy for His children.

GOD HAS COME NEAR TO US

There is a great difference between words and deeds. When someone makes a claim about himself, we want to see a follow-through in action. Most of us have experienced times when others said or promised they were going to help us, but when the time came for their assistance, they were nowhere to be found. We all know that it is easier to talk than to act.

But with God, you can count on His words being fulfilled through actions. He not only expressed concern for the Hebrews, He came down and delivered them. Whereas slavery and death are dominant ideas in Exodus chapters 1–2, the rest of the narrative changes to one of deliverance. For example, in Exodus 3:8, God says, "I have come down to deliver them out of the hand of the Egyptians, and to bring them up from that land to a good and large land, to a land flowing with milk and honey."

The relationship between God's attributes and His actions on behalf of the children of Israel and of us cannot be overemphasized. God is not capricious in His acts in the world; His actions consistently reflect what He is within Himself. In Exodus 3:8, the Lord says that His decision to come down to deliver the people relates to hearing their cries and knowing their sorrows. This does not mean that God Himself— dwelling above the universe, time, and space—experiences sorrow; but He surely knows our sorrows and desires to alleviate them.

The New Testament also provides a similar view of God. Jesus reveals the character of our heavenly Father in Matthew 6:

> Your Father knows the things you have need of before you ask Him.
>
> Therefore I say to you, do not worry about your life, what you will eat or what you will drink; nor about your body, what you will put on. Is not life more than food and the body more than clothing? Look at the birds of the air, for they neither sow nor reap nor gather into barns; yet your heavenly Father feeds them. Are you not of more value than they? Which of you by worrying can add one cubit to his stature?
>
> So why do you worry about clothing? Consider the lilies of the field, how they grow: they neither toil nor

spin; and yet I say to you that even Solomon in all his glory was not arrayed like one of these. Now if God so clothes the grass of the field, which today is, and tomorrow is thrown into the oven, will He not much more clothe you, O you of little faith?

Therefore do not worry, saying, "What shall we eat?" or "What shall we drink?" or "What shall we wear?" For after all these things the Gentiles seek. For your heavenly Father knows that you need all these things. But seek first the kingdom of God and His righteousness, and all these things shall be added to you (verses 8,25-33).

There are three major themes in that passage—God is fully aware of our needs, He is deeply concerned about taking care of us, and we must be committed to following His guidance for us to receive His benefits. He stands by at all times to come to our aid according to His purposes.

The greatest example of the sincerity of God to help us in our suffering is discovered in the incarnation of His Son, Jesus the Messiah. The overwhelming splendor of this is difficult to capture with human language, but the apostle Paul introduces us to a hymn sung in the early church in worship of the Son. After he urges the Christians at Philippi to do nothing through selfish ambition or conceit but to act for the benefit of others (Philippians 2:3-4), He sets forth Jesus, God in the flesh, as our example of selfless attitude and actions:

Consider this in yourselves what was also in Christ Jesus, who though existing in the form of God, did not consider being equal with God something to take advantage of, but He emptied Himself by taking the form of a bondservant, coming in the likeness of men. And being found in the form as a man, He humbled Himself and became obedient until death, even death of the cross (2:5-8, personal paraphrase).

Jesus is the surest proof that God truly does love and care for us, willing to meet us in our needs and take away the results of our personal failures as well as comfort us in the midst of a sinful world. Jesus was willing to suffer for us and with us; He is the personal face of the invisible and infinite God (John 14:9).

Chapter Six

Can God Experience Pain?

When two junior high kids, whom I'll call Mike and Mary, entered my (William's) junior high classroom each morning, I knew that my day would be both gratifying and frustrating. Gratifying because Mike would always say, "Hi, teacher! What do you want me to do today?" By contrast, Mary would sit, stare at her desk, not open her textbook, and not respond to any question or assignment. She would not even answer the principal when he asked her to accompany him to the office. In the only instance that she did respond, Mary stood up, grimaced, and with all the strength her slight frame could muster, kicked him very hard square in the shin!

In our studies, service, and worship, God wants us to be like Mike, and not Mary. A Christian who acts like Mike is eager to learn about God. Learning about God is important because He loves us and we love Him.

But as we will soon see in this chapter, getting to know God isn't always easy. There are some things about Him that are hard to understand. We cannot perfectly understand the infinite, as we are finite. But God certainly does reveal certain truths about Himself in the Bible, and it's good for us to know what He says so that we can relate to Him better. Among other things, God says He is...

1. Spirit (John 4:24)

2. invisible (Romans 1:20)

3. self-existent (John 5:26)

4. changeless (Malachi 3:3)

5. undivided (Deuteronomy 6:4)

6. truth (1 John 5:20)

7. omnipresent (existing everywhere) (Psalm 139:7)

8. almighty (Genesis 17:1)

9. all-knowing (Isaiah 46:9-10)

10. eternal (Psalm 90:2)

11. infinite (Psalm 139:1-6)

12. sovereign (Isaiah 46:10-11)

Knowing these qualities of God will have a positive impact on our worship of Him. The better we know Him, the better our worship. Unfortunately, many today have a wrong perspective of worship. The goal of worship should be to praise God, not to make us feel good. Isn't this the meaning of John 4:24? "Those who worship Him must worship in spirit and truth." Of this text commentator William Hendriksen wrote, "Such worship, therefore, will not only be spiritual instead of physical, inward instead of outward, but will also be directed to the true God as *set forth in Scripture*..."[1] (emphasis added). Were this true, our understanding of God as He is defined in Scripture is very much related to our worship.

A correct understanding of God also enhances our service to God. Part of that service may include learning about God or teaching about Him. Ephesians 4:11 states that God has given a variety of workers: apostles, prophets, evangelists, pastors, and teachers. Other areas of giftedness are mentioned in Romans 12, 1 Corinthians 12, and 1 Peter 4. These gifted ones serve God through their ministries. Others serve God by their faithful and diligent response to those who minister to them. We can broadly say that we serve God both by teaching and by learning.

Does this teaching and learning have a defined purpose? The answer is yes, according to Ephesians 4:13, which connects our unity with our knowledge of the Lord: "till we all come to the unity of the faith and of the knowledge of the Son of God..." The context of Ephesians 4:13 shows that the knowledge is mature, not elemental. It's God's purpose that we are established in our beliefs about Him through learning and teaching.

How does this relate to what we've been learning in this book? Well, we need to know if God can experience pain, or suffer, or experience feelings, because it will affect our understanding of Him and how we relate to Him.

A Word About God

Theology (our beliefs) is what we understand about God and how He relates to the universe.[2] In a way, Bible interpretation and theology are symbiotic. Our theology is formed by our Bible interpretation, but in turn our theology is a criterion for our interpretations of the Bible. In this chapter, we are going to discuss God's divine attributes as they relate to His suffering.

By divine attributes, we are referring to qualities that are essential to God and that constitute what God is.[3] Without such qualities, God would not be God.[4] These qualities are thought to inhere in the nature of God[5] or even be identical to that nature.[6]

For example, let's consider some related truths that are found in Isaiah 46:9-10; Matthew 10:30; John 16:30; 21:17; and Romans 11:33.

> I am God, and there is no other; I am God and there is none like Me, declaring the end from the beginning, and from ancient times things that are not yet done... the very hairs of your head are all numbered...Now we are sure that You know all things...Lord, You know all things...Oh, the depth of the riches both of the wisdom and knowledge of God!

Those quotations above, and others in Scripture, state that God knows everything. That is a quality of His being. God cannot know any more or any less than He does without altering that quality and thus changing His nature. From such texts as these a theological belief is formed by induction. That is, by looking at several biblical texts on the subject, we can conclude that God is omniscient (all-knowing). That conclusion then becomes a part of our belief system. And our belief system then becomes a method of interpreting Scripture about God.

Note that while our having a belief system is important, such a system is not infallible, so we need to always be willing to subject it to Scripture.

If, for example, we believe that God knows all, when we read of God walking through Eden after the Fall and asking, "Where are you?" (Genesis 3:9), we should not interpret that to mean God is ignorant of some things. Rather, we should interpret Genesis 3:9 according to our belief system, which has been informed by Scripture that God is omniscient.

Thus, our theology of God's omniscience controls our interpretation of Genesis 3:9. In similar ways, the understanding of this chapter's contents may aid us in Bible interpretation.

How Can God Suffer If He Is Perfect?

Now, if God is perfect, and He does not change, how is it that He *becomes* a sufferer or *ceases* to be a sufferer? He doesn't. It's important to realize that God *eternally* suffers. He does not suffer *temporally*. He eternally suffers our sufferings because He eternally knows of them.

Why is that distinction important? It is generally thought that God's qualities reside in God's nature. Without His qualities, God would not be God. If we have an understanding of God's nature that is compatible with the classical view of God, then we believe that God's nature does not "become" anything. If God is perfect, then God cannot either become a sufferer or cease to be a sufferer. If God is eternal and if He knows all, then, for example, God knows of and is excited about the birth of the Savior *in eternity*. God did not begin to become excited over Jesus' birth just before it happened.

But one might respond, "When looking at the Christmas story, we see evidences of God's becoming excited, do we not? God caused the star to appear. He spoke to Joseph of the birth of Jesus in a dream. He sent angels to announce that birth and to sing the glories of it. Doesn't that prove God became excited, in time, when Jesus was born?"

No, not necessarily. What these events demonstrate is that God *acts* in time to show to men His eternal feelings. That action in time doesn't mean that God just then began to be something He was not. It only shows that at the proper time, God demonstrated His excitement to His creation. As we discussed earlier, God works within our framework. As an infinite being, He is eternally excited, but He shows His excitement to us in our finite time frame.

Were God to have begun to be excited about Christ's birth when that birth occurred, then God's feelings would have been changing, and thus He would not already be perfect. And in the same way that His excitement over Christ's birth is eternal, His pain over our suffering is eternal. Our suffering does not cause God to begin to suffer. If we lose a loved one, or develop a terminal illness, or undergo some other tragedy, God suffers (is concerned) over that event in eternity. Of course God's feeling are displayed in time, but that does not make God's feelings temporally caused or any less eternal.

If God Is Unchangeable, How Can He Suffer?

Because God is perfect, He does not change. But if He doesn't change, how can we say He can suffer? The answer, of course, is that God suffers eternally. But unless creation is eternal too, how could God suffer eternally with His creatures? The obvious solution to some is that God does not just exist at the beginning *before* time; God exists also *in* and *after* time. No thing or experience is ever new to God. But we cannot just leave the issue of God's unchangeableness with that statement, because we still run into some difficulties with the doctrine of God's immutability, or His unchangeableness.

God does not change. That is a bold statement! What biblical evidence is there for that assertion? Quite a lot: "I am the Lord, I do not change" (Malachi 3:6); "the Father of lights, within whom there is no variation" (James 1:17); "God is not a man, that he...should change his mind" (Numbers 23:19 NIV); "the Glory of Israel does not...change his mind; for he is not a man..." (1 Samuel 15:29 NIV); "they will perish, but you will endure...they will be changed but You are the same" (Psalm 102:26-27); "the counsel of the LORD stands forever" (Psalm 33:11).

This quality of God has been defined by theologian Willam Shedd as "the unchangeableness of His essence, attributes, purposes, and consciousness."[7] Charles Hodge comments that God is unchangeable in His essence, attributes, plans, and purposes.[8] But the unchangeableness of God's will present some difficulty. For if God's will does not change at all, then how are we to understand such passages as, "So the LORD changed His mind" (Exodus 32:14 NASB); "the LORD regretted that He had made Saul king" (1 Samuel 15:35); "You are...One who relents" (Jonah 4:2).

Those last several verses may suggest to some that God changes His mind. I (William) rather think that we experience God's qualities in a similar way as I this morning experienced the sun during my walk. Most days, I walk briskly for 30 minutes for the health of my heart and to counter the effects of my diabetes. This January morning was cold. From time to time during my walk I enjoyed some warmth from the sun. But when I turned a corner, I walked into a shady area that was colder. Now, that didn't happen because the sun had moved. Rather, I had moved. Similarly, our relationship to God may be changed according to *our* movement—we move closer to God, or we move further away. This analogy fits Hodge's view that immutability does not mean immobility.[9] God may *seem* to treat an individual differently from day to day. But in actuality, it is the relationship that has changed, not God.

God's qualities do not change. The moral qualities of God include both a hatred of sin and a love of those who do righteousness: "The way of the wicked is an abomination to the LORD, but He loves him who follows righteousness" (Proverbs 15:9). These dispositions are changeless in God. But we may be experiencing one or the other of God's attitudes toward us depending on where we are walking.

If God Is Eternal, How Can He Suffer?

For us to try to understand what is meant by God's eternality, we might consider that time is a measure of the movement of things changeable. But because God is unchangeable, time does not measure Him. Time has a beginning and an end, but eternity has neither. God has no beginning or end; He is above time. Time has a before and after, but God has neither. So, God is not subject to time.[10]

But if God is eternal in this sense, one might ask why Scripture sometimes describes some aspect of God in temporal terms. Consider Romans 8:29: "Whom He foreknew, He also predestined..." Now, is this not correctly understood to mean that at one point in time God knew something in another point in time? I think instead that these sorts of texts are further examples of what E.W. Bullinger calls "anthropopatheia" or "condescension."[11]

We ascribe human characteristics to God, don't we? For example, in a worship song we might ask God to arise, but we know that God has no legs. In Matthew 18:10 Christ says that angels behold the face of the Father, but we know God is Spirit! (John 4:24). In Exodus 15:8 we read, "With the blast of Your nostrils the waters were gathered together." Yet we know that doesn't mean God has nose by which He works miracles. So when God is said in Romans 8:29 to foreknow, that is an attempt to describe God's infinity in terms that our limited minds can grasp.

We are changed by events in time, and thankfully, our pain is contained in time. But God is eternal and He knows our pain outside the boundaries of time.

In the summer of about 1960, a newlywed couple was on Highway 101 going from San Diego to Northern California for their honeymoon. The bride was a young Christian woman who had just "graduated" from our single young adult class at a large Baptist church. She was a tall, lovely girl with straight black hair. I do not recall knowing the bridegroom, as he was not a member of our church.

Surely this young couple was anticipating, while driving along the coast, many years of happy marriage. They probably discussed such things as careers, homes, and having children. Their future seemed certain to be one of long duration and genuine happiness derived from loving each other more and more over time.

If you are familiar with Highway 101, you will know the route has to be driven with extreme care because it runs alongside steep cliffs descending to the shore of the Pacific Ocean. That's why, according to the account the husband later told the girl's family, he did not at first agree to his bride's request that she be allowed to do some of the driving. She was an inexperienced driver and had just gotten her license to drive.

His new bride, however, became insistent, and so finally, weakened in his resolve, and against his better judgment, the husband pulled over to the side, stopped the car, and changed seats with her. She began the task of carefully negotiating those seemingly endless curves. But there was one curve she didn't manage.

The car broke through the guardrail and plummeted over the edge of the cliff to the rocks below. The husband survived the wreck, but his bride did not. The story has it that as the car tumbled down the cliff, the young woman, her hands vainly gripping hard the steering wheel, turned to her love and said, "I'm so sorry."

What could measure or contain the suffering of the bridegroom and of the family of the bride over this tragedy? I'm confident that although the event occurred so many years ago, those involved who are still alive still have sorrow over the death of their beloved whenever they think of it. So what can contain their sorrow? Time does! Because we live inside time, we experience events successively, meaning that one experience follows another.

We suffer in time, but God is not bound by time. Because God exists in eternity, if He suffers, He eternally suffers. His suffering has no beginning and no ending. From eternity God felt the anguish of the car on Highway 101 going over the cliff, and into eternity He does. This is our God, and we should appreciate who and what He is as we realize that He, in His being, because the quality of eternality resides in Him, suffers eternally when we suffer in time. Were this not true, then God would be changing. But God does not change.

Now, one may argue that God cannot act in time if He is eternal. Yet according to the Bible, God does act in time. Consider Galatians 4:4: "When the fullness of the time had come, God sent forth His Son." In the book *The Battle for God,* Norm Geisler and Wayne House respond that in the above argument, "there is a confusion between the eternal Actor (God) and His temporal actions...His acts are in time but His attributes are beyond time."[12] Well, okay, let's accept the idea that God, while in eternity, can cause things temporal. Even then, we may be left with some difficulty in understanding this concept of God existing *beyond* time but acting *in* time.

One example of where this problem might arise is in Colossians 2:9: "In Him [Christ] dwells all the fullness of the Godhead bodily." Here's the issue: If Christ is in time and God is in Christ, is not God also in time? Are not the divine attributes bound within time if the fullness of them is in Christ, who is in time? The scholar J.B. Lightfoot explains that Paul did not merely write "bodily," which would have confined the Godhead to the limits of space. Instead, Paul wrote "in bodily wise" meaning "in bodily manifestation."[13] God's attributes are seen in Christ yet not confined in Christ. This is God *acting* in time, not *limited* to time.

What Lightfoot appears to mean is that if God is everywhere, omnipresent, then God cannot be limited to existing in the body of Jesus. If God knows all, then God cannot be limited to the human understanding of Jesus, which increased in knowledge according to Luke 2:40,52. If God is all-powerful, omnipotent, then God cannot be tired at Jacob's well in John chapter 4. This is not saying that Christ is not God; this is saying that He is at the same time man too! Yet God made Himself known through the human nature by speaking the words and doing the works of God. And in that sense, the fullness of deity is seen "in bodily wise."

Those who argue that God is somehow bound within time point to 1 Corinthians 3:16, which says, "The Spirit of God dwells in you." The argument might be stated like this:

> The Spirit, who is God, is in the Christian.
> But, the Christian is in time.
> So, God is in time.

But the proponent of this argument has not completely grasped the consequences of such a conclusion. If God cannot be contained in all heaven and earth (1 Kings 8:27), how can He be contained in a Christian? It is better to understand that God being in us means that God is *acting* in time, not that God is *limited* to time. Perhaps that is where the misunderstanding occurs.

If God Is Transcendent, How Can He Suffer?

When used of God, the Word *transcendent* refers to the fact God is above and beyond His creation. Isaiah 57:15 says, "Thus says the High and Lofty One...I dwell in the high and holy place, with him who has a contrite and humble spirit."

Other Scriptures suggest God's transcendence as well: "The LORD is high above all nations" (Psalm 113:4); "I am from above...I am not of this world" (John 8:23); "Will God indeed dwell on the earth? Behold, heaven and the heaven of heavens cannot contain You" (1 Kings 8:27).

That raises a question: If God is so far beyond us, how can He suffer with us? The answer is that God, while above us, is also with us. This doctrine is called God's *immanence*. This also is taught in Scripture: "Where can I flee from Your presence? If I ascend into heaven, You are there; if I make my bed in hell, behold, You are there" (Psalm 139:7-8); "He is not far from each one of us; for in Him we live and move and exist" (Acts 17:27-28).

Some wrongly suggest that God's nature is divided, or that He has two natures. One nature of God is thought by some to be involved in the world, while the other is said not to be.[14] Yet Scripture does not attribute separate qualities to one nature or part of God and other qualities to another nature or part. Each of God's qualities is true of all of God. For example, all of God is everywhere, not just part of God. All of God is love, not just part of God. All of God is almighty, not just part of God.

There is no passage that says God is divided, with part of Him above and part of Him below. Instead Scripture teaches the unity, or simplicity, of God: "The LORD is one" (Deuteronomy 6:4); "the LORD our God, the LORD is one" (Mark 12:29).

So, the second portion of Isaiah 57:15—"I dwell...with him who has a contrite and humble spirit"—encourages us to believe that the very same God who is transcendent (beyond us) is also immanent (with us). That is how God shares in our sufferings. The doctrine, therefore, is very relevant to the theme of this book.

That God is immanent simply means that God is with us. This truth is so uncomplicated that a child can sing, "Jesus loves me, this I know" without understanding himself as Jesus. The child sings without thinking that he and God are one. Yet some people interpret God's nearness to mean that God *is* us. They say creation and God are one! Here are three examples:

In her book *Embraced by the Light,* Betty Eadie claims to have died during surgery. Her spirit went through a tunnel, she says, and into the spirit world, where she received many teachings. Then she was sent back to her physical existence in order to share these teachings with us. Eadie claims that in heaven she was taught that every religion is good and necessary.[15] Eadie also says that Jesus is not God.[16] Rather, she says that we are God. As Eadie puts it, "I felt God in the plant, in me, his love pouring into us. We were all one."[17] However, Eadie may have felt something other than God.

Then there is Shirley MacLaine's book *Out on a Limb.* She claims, without evidence, that the church Council of Nicaea in the fourth century removed texts from the Bible that plainly taught reincarnation.[18] There is no historical or manuscript evidence at all of this happening. The message of Christ, MacLaine explains, is how to accomplish the soul's progression to perfection.[19] MacLaine also declares, "You are God. You know you are divine...act accordingly."[20] As MacLaine's supposed "spirit guide," David, states, "It is part of every cell, it is part of DNA, it is in us, and all of us, and the whole of it—everywhere—is what we call 'God.'"[21] Yet none of this agrees with Scripture.

Finally, we come to James Van Praag, who has appeared on television to tell viewers how to communicate with their departed loved ones. In his book *Talking to Heaven,* Van Praag suggests a technique for chatting with the dead: Make a date with the dead person under a streetlight, ask questions of the dead person, and he or she will answer by blinking the streetlight "once for yes and twice for no."[22] Then Van Praag assures us, "You are invincible. You are truly God."[23] But one who is "truly God" would not be standing next to a streetlight waiting for it to blink!

Such thoughts, of course, are not scriptural. Not only do the above teachings fail to recognize the transcendence of God, they also misrepresent the immanence of God. Scripture says, "God *with* us," not "God *is* us"! At the same time, the Bible says that while God is far above us, He also is with us. That is why a transcendent God can suffer! In every pain we face, we experience God in His immanence. What a great God we have!

If God Is Impassible, How Can He Suffer?

Some people say that because God is impassible ("without passion"), and thus without feelings, then He cannot suffer. They might try to use Acts 17:25 to support their point, a passage that speaks of God's impassibility: "Nor is He worshiped with men's hands, as though He needed anything, since He gives to all life, breath, and all things."

But if God were without feelings, how could He suffer? The answer is that the bare definition of impassible is not the precise equivalent of the doctrine as taught by some theologians.

Theologian William Shedd says that impassibility means "the Divine nature cannot be caused to suffer from any external cause."[24] Geisler, another theologian, defines impassibility in a way similar to Shedd. He says that God's "feelings are not the result of actions imposed on Him by others. His feelings flow from His eternal and unchangeable nature."[25] Note that not all theologians agree with these definitions of impassibility.[26] Wayne Grudem, for example, wrongly defines impassibility as "God has no passions or emotions."[27] Because of his definition he does not affirm God's impassibility. And Clark Pinnock uses this definition to show that God is changeable.[28]

The difference, we see, between the unqualified definition of the word *impassibility* and Shedd's and Geisler's understanding of that doctrine is that while God suffers, He does not suffer as a result of things or events external to Himself. What God experiences eternally is caused by what God is, not by events in time. Neither Shedd nor Geisler deny that God suffers. Rather they say that creation, including man, cannot cause God to suffer. In other words, God only suffers from that which is in Himself.

This does not contradict the opinion expressed elsewhere in this book that God eternally suffers when we suffer. There is no contradiction because it is not elsewhere in this book affirmed that the reason God suffers is our suffering. God suffers because of what God is, not because of what creation is!

There are some who say that if Christ is God, then God cannot be made to suffer by men. But there's a problem with that. Perhaps you are among the many who saw Mel Gibson's film *The Passion of the Christ*. You may remember, as many do, being overcome with emotion at the sight of our Savior suffering so greatly from the scourging, the crown of thorns, and the spikes driven into His hands and feet. Some might say, "If we believe that Christ is God, then men cannot hurt God"? Didn't men hurt Christ? Yet I think those who caused Christ to suffer so greatly did not hurt God.

That may sound confusing, and in a later chapter, we will more fully consider the issue of Christ's humanity and deity and how the two natures in Christ should qualify our understanding of how the pain of the cross affected God. There we will try to provide support for the view that Christ experiences some things in His humanity that He does not experience in His deity. There are quite a few sound, conservative thinkers, among both ancients and moderns, who believe that God in Christ did not suffer from the scourging, crucifixion, and death because that suffering was experienced by Christ's humanity only.

But even if it is true that men did not cause God to suffer because Christ was crucified, that does not mean that God does not suffer. God is suffering when we suffer. But the point is that *men* do not cause His suffering. God's suffering is caused by His own nature.

Some people see another problem. It is asserted by them that God's impassibility is "in serious tension with the Biblical notion of divine love for the world."[29] Yet I think that God is not caused to love or to experience any other feeling or condition by creation; in that sense, we think God is impassible. The biblical notion of God's love is that God's love is not conditioned on what the world does but on what God is. God *is love* (1 John 4:8); He is not made loving by the world!

We believe the view that God's suffering is caused by God's nature best fits our understanding of God. If God is unchangeable, He cannot suffer more tomorrow than He ever has suffered. If God is perfect, then He cannot increase or decrease in suffering. God has decreed all that happens (Isaiah 46:10-11; Ephesians 1:11), but that decree does not include things in God as explained by the theologians Lewis Sperry Chafer[30] and Strong.[31] God does not decree Himself! Therefore, in my opinion, no event causes God suffering. In other words, all God's feelings are eternal, and so men do not cause them in time. Yes, God is passible, *if* that means having feelings. But nothing outside of God causes God's passion.

Every pain, all the suffering that we experience is experienced by God because of what He is. What a great God we have!

> You, Lord, in the beginning laid the foundation of the
>   earth,
> And the Heavens are the works of Your hands;
> They will perish, but You remain;
> And they all will become old like a garment,
> And like a mantle You will roll them up;
> Like a garment they will also be changed.
> But You are the same,
> And Your years will not come to an end (Hebrews
>   1:10-12).

Chapter Seven

Did God Suffer When Christ Died on the Cross?

His divine nature which alone was
passionless remained void of passion...
we say that God suffered in the flesh, but never
that His divinity suffered in the flesh, or that
God suffered through the flesh.

—John of Damascus,
"Exposition of the Orthodox Faith,"
Chapter XXVI

Christians affirm that God came into this world in the person of Jesus the Messiah to save His people from their sins (Matthew 1:21; John 3:16). The apostle John, probably more than any of the other evangelists, indicated in the first chapter of his Gospel that the *Logos,* or Word, who existed before all time and the Creator of all things (John 1:1-3) became a human being and dwelt among us (John 1:14).

The apostle Paul continued this theme in his letters, indicating that God sent His Son, born of a woman and born under the law (Galatians 4:4), and that Jesus, though God, humbled Himself by taking the form of a human to die on the cross (Philippians 2:8).

Evangelical theologians, in concert with the church for the last

2000 years, stand together on the truths of the preceding paragraphs. At the same time, there have been differences regarding the statement that God took upon Himself humanity and suffered for us. In order to more clearly explain the matter of Jesus' sacrifice, it would be well for us to consider the biblical teachings about His deity, humanity, and the incarnation.

Jesus Is God and Man

It is clear that Scripture explicitly teaches that Jesus the Messiah is God in the same manner and to the same extent that the Father and the Holy Spirit are God. There are a number of proof texts for this in the New Testament.

Christ Does the Works of God and Man

We ascribe the work of creation to God because we are told that God is the Creator in the very first verse of Scripture: "In the beginning God created..." (Genesis 1:1). Nowhere in Scripture are we told that anyone except God created. The psalmist too affirms that God alone is the Creator:

> Long ago you laid earth's foundations, the heavens are the work of your hands. They pass away but you remain; they all wear out like a garment, like outworn clothes you change them; but you never alter, and your years never end (Psalm 102:25-27 NJB).

The apostle Paul identifies Jesus as the one about whom the psalmist speaks:

> He has delivered us from the power of darkness and conveyed us into the kingdom of the Son of His love... For by Him all things were created that are in heaven and that are on earth, visible and invisible, whether thrones or dominions or principalities or powers. All things were created through Him and for Him (Colossians 1:13,16).

The apostle John also indicates that Jesus, the Word, is responsible for everything that has been made: "All things were made through Him, and without Him nothing was made that was made" (John 1:3).

If only God created, and if Christ is Creator, then Christ is God.

Other works of Christ argue for His deity with similar efficiency: Christ upholds the universe (Colossians 1:17), He judges the world (John 5:27-29), and He forgives sins (Mark 2:5-7). Neither the most powerful angel nor the most blessed man is capable of doing what God does. Christ does these things, however, indicating that Christ is truly God.

But note that Christ Jesus also possesses the attributes of humanity: He is temporal. Because Jesus was born as a human, He cannot be eternal and Creator and immutable. Thus, it is scriptural to apply one set of works and qualities to one of Christ's natures that cannot be applied to the other.

Christ Has the Attributes of God and Man

The deity of Jesus is also demonstrated by certain attributes that He possesses, attributes that only God has. One is that God is omniscient, or all-knowing. The prophet Isaiah seems to make this attribute a test of deity in Isaiah chapters 21–48, and challenges false deities to prove themselves by this capacity.

> Let them bring forth and declare to us what is going to take place…Or announce to us what is coming; declare the things that are going to come afterward, that we may know you are gods…[41:22-23]. Who among them can declare this and proclaim to us the former things? [43:9]. Who is like Me? Let him proclaim and declare it; Yes, let him recount it to Me in order…And let them declare to them all the things that are coming and the events that are going to take place [43:7]. I am the LORD, and there is no other [45:5]. For I am God and there is no other; I am God, and there is no one like Me, declaring the end from the beginning [46:9-10] (NASB).

How much more clear could Isaiah be? God knows all, and only He does. Jesus is able to pass this very test.

The apostle John records these words from the disciples of Christ:

> See, now You are speaking plainly, and using no figure of speech! Now we are sure that You know all things, and have no need that anyone should question You. By this we believe that You came forth from God (John 16:29-30).

Peter by himself confesses the same in John 21:17: "Lord, You know all things." Later the apostle Paul makes the same observation, saying that in Christ "are hidden all the treasures of wisdom and knowledge" (Colossians 2:3).

Even though Christ is all-knowing, which affirms His deity, He also has limitations in His knowledge, as evidenced by the following passages:

> Of that day and hour no one knows, not even the angels in heaven, nor the Son, but only the Father (Mark 13:32).

> Jesus increased in wisdom and stature, and in favor with God and men (Luke 2:52).

So, some things that are true of one nature in Christ are not true of the other nature in Christ.

Christ Receives the Honors of God and Endures Humiliation as a Man

God, rightly, will not share His glory: "I will not give My glory to another" (Isaiah 48:11). Only God is to be worshipped and served (Matthew 4:10). How is it, then, that Christ has God's glory (John 17:5), is to be worshipped (Matthew 28:9; Philippians 2:10), and is to be served (Colossians 3:24)? These passages are affirmations that Christ is God.

As God, Christ is to be exalted above all. But as a man, Christ was humiliated by other men, as Philip the evangelist explained to the Ethiopian eunuch:

> The place in the Scripture which he read was this: "He was led as a sheep to the slaughter; and as a lamb before its shearer is silent, so He opened not His mouth. In His humiliation His justice was taken away, and who will declare His generation? For His life is taken from the earth" (Acts 8:32-33).

This humbling of Christ extended to being a servant and even dying on a cross:

> Although [Christ] existed in the form of God, [He] did not regard equality with God a thing to be grasped, but emptied Himself, taking the form of a bond-servant, and being made in the likeness of men. Being found in appearance as a man, He humbled Himself by becoming obedient to the point of death, even death on a cross (Philippians 2:6-8 NASB).

Other Evidence of Christ's Deity and Humanity

Christ is on an equal footing with God, yet He was but a servant in His humanity. He is given divine names such as Yahweh (Philippians 2:11), and the I AM (John 8:58), but He had the common Jewish name of *Jesus*. His name is mentioned occurring alongside the Father and the Holy Spirit's (Matthew 28:19; 1 Corinthians 1:13; 2 Corinthians 13:14), and yet He is treated as a common criminal by the Jews and the Romans. He is declared by the writer to the Hebrews be the exact image of God (Hebrews 1:10-12), but He is also in the form and likeness of man (Philippians 2:8), in human flesh (John 1:14).

Multiple passages explicitly state that Jesus is God and man. First, let's see where He is called God:

In the beginning was the Word, and the Word was with God, and the Word was God (John 1:1 NASB).

No one has seen God at any time; the only begotten God who is in the bosom of the Father, He has explained Him (John 1:18 NASB).

Thomas answered and said to Him, "My Lord and my God!" (John 20:28 NASB).

...whose are the fathers, and from whom is the Christ according to the flesh, who is over all, God blessed forever. Amen (Romans 9:5 NASB).

...looking for the blessed hope and the appearing of the glory of our great God and Savior, Christ Jesus (Titus 2:13 NASB).

Of the Son He says, "Your throne, O God, is forever and ever, and the righteous scepter is the scepter of His kingdom. You have loved righteousness and hated lawlessness; therefore God, Your God, has anointed You with the oil of gladness above Your companions." And, "You, Lord, in the beginning laid the foundation of the earth, and the heavens are the works of Your hands" (Hebrews 1:8-10 NASB).

Jesus is also called a man:

Jesus came out, wearing the crown of thorns and the purple robe. And Pilate said to them, "Behold the Man!" (John 19:5).

The Jews answered Him, saying, "For a good work we do not stone You, but for blasphemy, and because You, being a Man, make Yourself God" (John 10:33).

When the Son of God entered into human existence, He did not cease being God. Unfortunately, some evangelical theologians seem to say that Jesus lost access to some divine attributes when He became a man. For example, Millard Erickson believes that Jesus lost access to the infinite knowledge of God in the incarnation,[1] or became as ignorant as we are in most matters,[2] or "accepted limitations on the functioning of His divine attributes."[3] For Jesus to stop using a divine attribute is for Him to stop being divine! One who begins to be ignorant is no longer omniscient. One who begins a confinement in a body is no longer omnipresent. One whose strength is limited to muscles and tendons is no longer omnipotent.

God does not change. Exercising, not just possessing, divine attributes is what makes God God. Anyone who would aver that Jesus lost something when He took on manhood misunderstands the relationship of the human and divine in one person. For Jesus to *exist* in a human body is not the same thing as saying He is *limited* to a human body. When the person Jesus was in the manger in Bethlehem, with all of the limitations of being human, He was simultaneously the almighty God over the universe—two natures in one person. When Jesus said that He did not know the time of His coming (Mark 13:32), at the same time He was the wisdom and knowledge of God (Colossians 2:3)—two natures in one person. The Son of God exists both inside and outside of His humanity. Christ, as God, is more than He is as a man. John Calvin forcefully explains this relationship of the divine and human in Jesus:

> Another absurdity which they obtrude upon us [is] that if the Word of God became incarnate, it must have been enclosed in the narrow tenement of an earthly body, is sheer petulance. For although the boundless essence of the Word was united with human nature into one Person, we have no idea of any enclosing. The Son of God descended miraculously from heaven, *yet without abandoning heaven;* was pleased to be conceived miraculously in the virgin's womb, to live on the earth, and hang upon a cross, and yet *always filled the world as from the beginning.*[4]

The understanding of the divine and human nature in the person of Jesus, as expressed by Calvin, is consistent with how this has been understood by the church over the centuries,[5] and is most consistent with the teaching of the biblical text.

The Union of Two Natures in One Person

Certainly the fact that Christ is somehow both God and man is not hard to say or to grasp at an elemental level, and is believed by most who call themselves Christians. All evangelical thinkers will agree with the basic statement that Christ is God and man. The more difficult issue is to conceive, and then to explain, how Jesus is two natures in one person, and that God is somehow three persons in one nature.

In considering this, there are several issues to examine: (1) whether Christ, in becoming man, changed any detail, even minutely, associated with His being God; (2) what constitutes Christ's humanity, or how human is He; (3) how His deity and His humanity, each of which are called natures, function or are used together to comprise only one person; and (4) who is the subject of the experiencing, willing, knowing, and doing of the humanity of Christ.

Why is this important? Jesus is at the very center of our Christian faith, and to comprehend salvation and God's sufficiency to save requires that we understand the person of the Christ. In spite of this, many Christians have made little effort to define Him. This certainly would be understandable were it the case that the writers of Scripture did not provide details about Christ's person, but they have. Moreover, while we must applaud all sincere efforts to follow Christ in how we live, we also should do what we can to understand the one whom we are following. Though many of the theological questions are difficult to answer, they are nonetheless essential to understanding our faith and our salvation. All of this becomes very important because people regularly use inaccurate terms, illustrations, and sloppy language when they speak about how Jesus is fully God and fully man.

For example, it is not uncommon to hear one say that Jesus is the

God-man. Yet such is not true, for this would be a third reality, a new nature with a mixture of God and man, which is the heresy of Eutychianism. Rather, Jesus the Son is fully God and fully man in one person. He is God and man, one person in two natures.

Also, you may hear someone say that God died on the cross for us. Now, if that person means that the one who is God died on the cross in His human nature, he is correct. But the nature of God cannot die or experience change. So let's further discuss God's immutability and impassibility.

Understanding God's Immutability and Impassibility

The Immutability of God

In chapters 5 and 6 we addressed God's immutability, or changelessness. But we must now consider this attribute as it relates to the incarnation of God. The fourth-century church father, St. Augustine, said, "...that which is changed does not retain its own being."[6] This is affirmed by the writer of Hebrews, who contrasted God with changeable creation: "They will be changed, but You are the same" (Hebrews 1:12).

What happened in the incarnation? When God entered into human existence, the Creator into His creation, did anything change in God? Was there a *loss* of anything that had been true of God prior to becoming a human, and was there any *addition* to God's being due to His assuming human nature? Because God is perfect, and nothing can be added to nor taken away from a perfect being (or in fact the being would not be perfect but lacking), the incarnation could not have added or subtracted anything from God's nature.

We must contend, then, that there was no change in God when Jesus became a man. If God is unchangeable, then the incarnation is not a change in God's nature, though it may be an addition to the person who has the nature of God. In the incarnation, God does not become a man, nor is the man God; the person, however, is God and man.

Because God is unchangeable, God's nature does not change into man's nature, and man's nature does not become God's nature. The incarnation is not God the Son losing, in any manner, the divine nature or qualities or even the use of such.

That's why I can suggest that all the limitations of Christ—such as His not knowing something, or sleeping in a boat, or growing and maturing, or getting tired or suffering on the cross—be understood to be occurring only in the humanity of Christ and not in His deity. That, in turn, affects the answer to the question posed in this chapter about the sense in which God suffered on the cross.

The Impassibility of God

If Christ died on the cross for our sins, and if He is God, then how can it be that God did *not* die on the cross? Much of the difficulty with understanding this dilemma comes from failing to distinguish the nature of the Son as God from the nature of the Son as man. We must not confuse the *natures* of Jesus—human and divine—with the *person* of Jesus. The person existed only as God in eternity, but there was an addition to the person, not the nature, when He became man. Since the divine nature of Jesus is eternal, infinite, immutable, and impassible, the nature cannot die nor suffer on the cross. On the other hand, the human nature of Jesus was subject to time, change, and pain, which meant that He could die and suffer on the cross.

At issue are these two questions: (1) What is meant when we say Christ is a man? (2) Can Christ as man experience what Christ as God cannot? These are the questions we will endeavor to answer in this chapter.

It is not unusual to have a person challenge this understanding of the nature of Jesus and His work on the cross. For example, recently a Mormon asked a young friend of mine (William), "How can God forsake God?" This is not an unfair question, because when Jesus was on the cross, Scripture addresses it: "He cried out with a loud voice, saying, 'Eli, Eli, lama sabachthani?' that is, 'My God, My God, why have You forsaken Me?'" (Matthew 27:46).

So the Mormon's question is a reasonable one—one that sincere believers might ask, as well as cultists who attempt to raise doubts about the nature of Christ. How can we assert that Jesus suffered and died on the cross as God, and also that God turned His back on Jesus? The answer is that the person who existed before time began added to His person humanity without ceasing to be deity. His divine and human nature are not mixed together; they each maintained the integrity of their respective properties. In His humanity the person who is the Son did not know everything, became tired, felt pain, was at only one place at a time, and experienced all the other limitations and attributes of a human. The person of the Son, by contrast, knows all things, is inexhaustible, does not temporally suffer, is everywhere, and experiences no limitations, expressing all the infinitude and attributes of God.

How can Jesus distinguish Himself from God if He is God? How can God pray to God, or God obey God?[7] Not only is the Son, as God, distinct in person from the other persons of the Trinity who share that same identical deity and share it equally, but Christ, in addition to being God, is also distinct from Himself as man. By this we mean that in certain manners, not only is Christ distinct from the Father and the Spirit; the deity of Christ also is distinct from, but not separate from, the humanity of Christ. As God, He is greater than Himself as man, just as Augustine stated.[8]

We are convinced that God's Son can experience, think, will, and act in His humanity in distinction from, but not in separation from, His deity. As a man, Jesus, the one who is the omnipotent God, required rest at Jacob's well. As God He is all-knowing, but as man He did not know many things. As God He is eternal, but as man He was conceived in Mary and born in time. As God He is impassible, but as man He suffers. One cannot put a nail in a divine nature or scourge a divine nature. And a divine nature cannot feel the weight of a cross. These can be done only to a human nature. Nonetheless, the person experienced all of this in His humanity.

Gregory of Nyssa, a fourth-century father of the church, in a statement equally powerful to John Calvin's, set forth the total divine and human nature of Jesus, each operating in their respective spheres in one person:

> How does [Apollinarius] deal with the breast, the swaddling clothes, life which grows and decays, the body's progressive growth, sleep, labor, parental obedience, trouble, grief, desire to eat the Passover supper, request for water, desire for food, chains, blows on the face, stripes from scourging, thorns on the head, the scarlet cloak, violence by [striking with] the reed, bitter wrath, vinegar, nails, spear, the fine garment, burial, tomb, and the stone? *How can such attributes belong to God?*...Tell me, who is ignorant? Who is afflicted by sadness? Who is constricted by weakness? Who cried out and was forsaken by God if the Father and the Son are one God? And who experienced abandonment when crying out on the cross?...How can the one divine substance be divided in suffering...[it is] our corporeal condition which is subject to passion, whereas eternal glory is immortal and *free from passion.*[9]

Consequently, when we say that God does not suffer when we suffer or when Jesus suffered on the cross, we are *not* saying that God is not at all experiencing passion or is unconcerned about us. God eternally suffers in Christ because the suffering of Christ is eternal in God's mind: "Him, being delivered by the determined purpose and foreknowledge of God..." (Acts 2:23); "...redeemed with...the precious blood of Christ, as of a lamb without blemish and without spot. He was indeed foreordained before the foundation of the world" (1 Peter 1:18-20). God does not live in time, and so God did not begin to suffer over the passion of His Son just at the time Christ died for us.

Remember that God is eternally all-knowing and does not acquire any new knowledge. He always knows all because He is perfect. Consequently, as Peter implies in Acts and in his first letter, God timelessly is aware of the sacrifice of Christ. We cannot suggest that God's suffering over the death of His Son lags behind His knowledge of it. God learns nothing new and so cannot suffer because of events caused by men that occur within the boundaries of time. Because God always knew of Christ's passion, and in fact predestined that passion, God always suffers because of the cross. To say differently denies that God is both eternal and omniscient.

In conclusion, then, did God experience the sufferings of Jesus on the cross? No, each of us can only experience our own suffering. Did He hurt and empathize for His Jesus on the cross? Yes, He did but not in time; He has had this concern for all eternity. God decreed the cross. Jesus has been the sacrificial Lamb of God from all eternity. This panged God's heart from all eternity. And the same is true about all of our pain, struggles, persecutions. All of our suffering has been on God's mind and in His heart from all eternity. He loves us with an unfathomable and eternal love.

If Christ as God exists in manners that He as man does not, and as man exists in manners that He as God does not, then as man He may experience passion that He as God does not experience. Only as man may He be under great emotional stress in Gethsemane. Only as man may He feel the whip and the thorns and the nails driven against and into His flesh. Only as man on the cross may He feel forsaken by His Father. Only as man may He die to redeem us.

Only as man He does these things!

Part Three:

Dealing with Pain in
Our Christian Walk

Chapter Eight

How Do We Participate in Christ's Sufferings?

In Colossians 1:24, the apostle Paul makes a somewhat puzzling comment. He said, "I now rejoice in my sufferings for you, and fill up in my flesh what is lacking in the afflictions of Christ." To an evangelical believer who believes that we cannot do any good works that make us deserving of salvation and that Jesus paid the entire debt for our sin on the cross, Paul's statement is difficult to understand.

Did Jesus fail to fully suffer for us? And even if that were the case, how can a mere human being, albeit an apostle, accomplish the fullness for sin that Jesus could not perform? And, are we also able to participate in the sufferings of Christ?

As we attempt to discern what Paul meant by his comment in Colossians 1:24, we will examine how Paul fulfilled this passage through his sufferings on behalf of his testimony for Christ, and how Epaphroditus did similarly by suffering for the members of Christ's body. We will also look at various New Testament texts about suffering for and with Christ.

Completing the Afflictions of Christ

Colossians 1:24 may seem problematic. After all, it is Christ who suffered for the church, not Paul. It is Christ who gave Himself for our sins (Galatians 1:4), not Paul.

Neither is the suffering of Christ for the salvation of men lacking. Christ paid the full price for our sin, and there remains no more payment to be made. "He, having offered one sacrifice for sins for all time, sat down at the right hand of God" (Hebrews 10:12 NASB). Only the personal exercising of faith in Christ is yet required for individual forgiveness of sins. The apostle Paul wrote,

> To him who does not work but believes on Him who justifies the ungodly, his faith is accounted for righteousness...[He] was delivered up because of our offenses, and was raised because of our justification. Therefore, having been justified by faith, we have peace with God through our Lord Jesus Christ (Romans 4:5,25–5:1).

Interpretations that Have Been Offered

There are a number of ways Colossians 1:24 has been interpreted. The main views are as follows:

1. There is something lacking in Christ's vicarious death for our sin that Paul intends to provide.

2. The apostle's meaning is that he suffers *with* Christ.

3. The meaning is only that his sufferings are similar to Christ's sufferings.

4. Paul is referring to the mystical union Christians have with Christ.[1]

5. Similar to view 4 is the view that when members of Christ's body (the church) suffer, then Christ suffers. That's why the ascended Christ asks the persecutor of the church, Paul, "Why are you persecuting Me?"[2]

6. Paul is talking about the sufferings of Messiah in the last days.[3]

7. Some have suggested that the afflictions of Christ refer

not to Jesus' redemptive sufferings but to His ministerial ones, and it is these that Paul is completing.[4]

8. Paul is speaking only of the suffering that comes from being associated with Christ.

Each of the above-suggested interpretations has some difficulties with it, and we will consider each one as to the likelilhood of its correctness after we have examined the occasion for Paul's comments and the terminology employed by him.

Evaluation of the Different Interpretations

The first view seems objectionable because even in the book of Colossians, Paul wrote that Christ's atonement is sufficient to save (1:20-22; 2:10,13). While the second view carries with it the truth that Christians suffer for Christ, such would not seem to include the idea of suffering *with* Christ, which Colossians 1:24 seems to be saying. While the third view is grammatically possible, being based on a certain understanding that the genitive case of the original ("afflictions *of* Christ") can mean a comparison between Paul's suffering and Christ's, that would still leave the problem of how Paul's sufferings are "filling up" that which "is lacking."

The fourth and fifth views have the advantage of referencing a true, and much-repeated New Testament doctrine that Christians are somehow *in* Christ. Yet views 4 and 5 still, unless more fully developed, leave unanswered how Christ's afflictions are in any way insufficient and how they are incomplete. The sixth view would, of course, require that Paul understood himself to be in the last days. Unless it is further developed, it still leaves unanswered the matter of how Paul fills up what is missing in the afflictions of Christ.

Last, we arrive at views 7 and 8. The strength of view 7, in our opinion, comes both from the meaning of the term "afflictions," as defined above, and from the context of Colossians 1:24. The meaning would be that Paul, and by extension Christians, complete Christ's afflictions when we minister to others. View 8 also has strength in that

Christ Himself promised suffering would come to those associated with His name (Matthew 10:16-22). Surely Paul is a vivid example of this suffering. However, neither of these views is sufficient by itself. Therefore, we take Colossians 1:24 to mean that Paul (and by extension, all Christians) suffer both from sacrificing for others and on behalf of Christ through persecution. This view has support from parallel passages of Scripture.

In many Scripture passages, Christians are called to deny themselves. Jesus said, "If anyone desires to come after Me, let him deny himself, and take up his cross daily, and follow Me. For whoever desires to save his life will lose it, but whoever loses his life for My sake will find it" (Matthew 16:24-25).

While we are called to sacrifice ourselves, Jesus also promised that all who trust in Him will find comfort. He said, "Come to Me, all you who labor and are heavy laden, and I will give you rest. Take My yoke upon you and learn from Me, for I am gentle and lowly in heart, and you will find rest for your souls. For My yoke is easy and My burden is light" (Matthew 11:28-30). This is not a promise of a life without trouble. Jesus also said there would be a cost for following Him: "You will be hated by all for My name's sake" (Matthew 10:22).

Part of denying ourselves is living in service to others. Jesus said that others will know we are His disciples if we love one another (John 13:35). He also said to put others first—in Luke 22:24 He said,

> The kings of the Gentiles exercise lordship over them, and those who exercise authority over them are called "benefactors." But not so among you; on the contrary, he who is greatest among you, let him be as the younger, and he who governs as he who serves. For who is greater, he who sits at the table, or he who serves? Is it not he who sits at the table? Yet I am among you as the One who serves (Luke 22:25-27).

We see here that Jesus is our example of a servant. Paul also taught us to serve each other: "Let nothing be done through selfish ambition or conceit, but in lowliness of mind let each esteem others better than himself. Let each of you look out not only for his own interests, but also for the interests of others" (Philippians 2:3-4).

Considerations for Understanding the Passage

So, some significant questions come to the surface with Colossians 1:24 in mind:

1. Given the above statements as to the completion of Christ's atoning work, how does the inspired apostle Paul speak of his own suffering for the church as his *completing* Christ's afflictions? And just as important for us,

2. Should we today suppose that we should, as did Paul, somehow "complete" Christ's afflictions? And,

3. If we should, how is this accomplished?

To answer these questions, we need to look a bit closer at the Colossians text to (1) understand the occasion for the writing of the words in question; (2) the terminology used; and (3) the likelihood of which interpretation of the passage is correct in view of these factors.

Occasion of Paul's Comments

You probably already know that the apostle Paul was imprisoned in Rome at the time he composed his letter to the Colossians. He was confined to his lodging and was chained to guards who watched him in four-hour shifts.[5] Paul found himself in that circumstance because of his zealous missionary activities for Christ. It was for Christ that Paul was a prisoner. And it is the apostle's reason for, and disposition during, his imprisonment that are vital to our comprehension of how we may emulate the apostle's purposeful suffering and the meaning of Colossians 1:24.

Paul's letter to the Colossians was "occasional"—by this we mean that Paul was motivated to write because of specific historical circumstances. In this case, Epaphras had arrived in Rome (1:7-8) to inform Paul of a heresy being taught in the church at Colossae. This heresy is defined by the points made in the letter by the apostle.

So, instead of dwelling on the uncomfortable circumstances of his own predicament, Paul focuses on the doctrinal wavering and spiritual needs of the church at Colossae. Rather than being absorbed by his own difficulties, Paul instead focuses on the theological and practical aberrations being fed to the Colossians. He composes this letter to counter the effects of heretical teachers. Paul's objective, then, is to serve the church and the cause of Christ even from prison. We don't see any concern about escape or easing his own afflictions.

So as Paul writes Colossians, his motive is driven by their need, not his own. Participating in Christ's sufferings involves being concerned and doing something about the welfare of others! It means focusing on the needs of our fellow believers, neighbors, or even the world population, and it means trying to do something to alleviate those destitutions.

For example, each year at Summit Ministries in Manitou Springs, Colorado, the young people who attend the seven two-week sessions on worldviews raise money for the poor and oppressed in the Sudan, in Africa. Probably few if any of these hundreds of young people will ever meet a person from the Sudan, and probably none of them will travel to the Sudan. Nonetheless, they provide thousands of dollars of relief each year to the starving and persecuted people in Sudan who are victims of Islamic fundamentalist persecution. These young people are extensions of the concerns of Jesus, filling up the afflictions of Christ that He never experienced.

But let's return to the meaning of Colossians 1:24. As we said earlier, this text is problematic. So, we should not be surprised to find experts disagreeing on how it should be interpreted. I (Wayne) will reiterate the several views mentioned earlier, and then give what I believe is the most plausible.

Understanding Paul's Terminology

In order to better understand Paul's teaching here, we need to examine the terms he used. The Greek noun for "sufferings" (*patheema*) is used in the New Testament to refer to general suffering (Romans 8:18), to Christ's redemptive suffering (Hebrews 2:10; 1 Peter 5:1), *and* for the suffering that Paul and Christians may endure for Christ:

> ...that I may know Him, and the power of His resurrection and the fellowship of His sufferings, being conformed to His death (Philippians 3:10).

> Beloved, do not be surprised at the fiery ordeal among you, which comes upon you for your testing, as though some strange thing were happening to you; but to the degree that you share the sufferings of Christ, keep on rejoicing, so that also at the revelation of His glory you may rejoice with exultation (1 Peter 4:12-13 NASB).

Going back to Colossians 1:24, the phrase "For the sake" (Greek, *huper*) is the same preposition commonly used by New Testament writers to define the purpose of the redemptive suffering of Christ for the elect. It often is translated "for." "This is My body which is given for you" (Luke 22:19); "I lay down My life for the sheep" (John 10:15); "Christ died for the ungodly" (Romans 5:6); "...who gave Himself for our sins" (Galatians 1:4); "Since Christ suffered for us..." (1 Peter 4:1).

So, it would appear that the apostle intends to mean that as Christ suffered for the church, so also does Paul. Paul's suffering for the church, while not redemptive (that is, it is not a price paid for the salvation of believers), yet involves his suffering to apply the merits of Christ's redemption to those who hear Paul and who read his letters.

The verb "filling up" (Greek, *antanapleeroo*) in Colossians 1:24 is in the present tense, denoting an ongoing action. Paul, in his imprisonment, and even perhaps in composing his letter, is doing this "filling up." The term is used nowhere else in the New Testament, but to "complete" something is an acceptable translation.[6]

Paul also uses the noun "lacking" (Greek, *hustereema*). To make a reference to something "lacking" is not an uncommon usage (see Luke 22:35; 1 Corinthians 12:24). In Mark 10:21 we read, "Looking at him, Jesus felt a love for him and said to him, 'One thing you lack: go and sell all you possess and give to the poor, and you shall have treasure in heaven; and come, follow Me.'"

We don't see how the meaning of Colossians 1:24 can easily exclude the idea that Paul is providing some of that which is needed to make Christ's afflictions complete. But we confess that this idea is somewhat new to us and that we had not thought much about the possibility of our own efforts as being a "filling up" of what is "lacking" in Christ's afflictions. Yet how, if Christ's redemptive work is in fact completed by His death and resurrection, can Paul or any of us possibly supply anything lacking in that? Perhaps the meaning of the term "afflictions" in Colossians 1:24 provides some insight.

The word "afflictions" (Greek, *thlipsis*) may provide a clue toward understanding Paul's intent in Colossians 1:24. Certainly "afflictions" and "sufferings" may be synonyms, but the usage of only the latter in the New Testament to indicate *Jesus' experience* on the cross lends credence to the view that in 1:24 the apostle uses the two nouns with *different meanings*. That which is lacking is not said to be in the "sufferings" of Christ, but in the "afflictions" of Christ. What distinction might Paul be intending by his use of two different nouns? Whereas "suffering" is used of Christ's passion for us, "affliction" never is!

The Greek word *thlipsis* is sometimes translated "tribulation," which is said to be the lot of Christians (see Matthew 24:9; John 16:33; Romans 12:12; Ephesians 3:13; 2 Thessalonians 1:4). So it seems likely to us that Paul is saying that his *suffering* for others is completing Christ's afflictions. The context (verses 23 and 25) indicates that Paul's ministry to others is connected to his suffering. And this is, in part, suggestive of how we may complete Christ's afflictions; that is, we may do that in our various ministries to the needs of others.

Let's look at more terms in Colossians 1:24:

Paul said that the location of our suffering is in our flesh (Greek, *sarki*). "Flesh" may refer to human nature (Romans 1:3), mankind in general (Matthew 24:22), the fallen, sinful nature (Galatians 5:17) or to one's body (1 Corinthians 15:39). The last would be Paul's meaning in Colossians 1:24. The same noun is used in Colossians 1:22 to reference Christ's suffering in His body. Consequently we may suppose that physical suffering for Christ or His people might be a ministry by which one may complete the afflictions of Christ.

The phrase "for the sake of" (Greek, *huper*) is a preposition that may be rendered "on behalf of." Paul's suffering in his body is said to be for the church. And the word "body" (Greek, *soma*) is often used metaphorically of the church, the body of Christ. In the Pauline letters, Christ is the head, and Christians are the body (see 1 Corinthians 12:12-27; Ephesians 1:23; 4:4,12,16; Colossians 1:18; 2:17; 3:15). As for the word "church" (Greek, *ekklesia*), this, of course, is the term used for both local assemblies (2 Corinthians 8:1; Colossians 4:16; Philemon 2) and the universal church (1 Corinthians 11:32; Galatians 1:2; Ephesians 5:27).

In summary, we believe that Paul, in Colossians 1:24, is saying that his sufferings for the church are providing some of what is "lacking" in the afflictions of Christ, taking those afflictions to be whatever is involved in the application of the effects of the redemptive suffering of our Lord. So, one such effect is that God promises to meet the needs of His people. Paul was, and we too, may be channels of God's provision, and as such may be required to suffer in one way or another.

So that we can better understand this concept, let's look at a parallel passage, 2 Corinthians 1:5. Sometimes a difficult passage may be clarified by another passage that talks about the same idea, but in greater detail. Such is the case here—in 2 Corinthians 1:5 Paul wrote, "As the sufferings of Christ abound in us, so our consolation also abounds through Christ."

Bible scholar A.T. Robertson saw "sufferings" in 2 Corinthians 1:5 as referring to Christ's own sufferings, or the sufferings that Christ endured, which we "carry around" in this life so that we may also make known Christ's resurrection (2 Corinthians 4:10). But this interpretation doesn't seem to fit well with the context.

Here, Paul seems to be speaking of the suffering he is enduring, on behalf of Christ, for others. He wrote, "Now if we are afflicted, it is for your consolation and salvation, which is effective for enduring the same sufferings which we also suffer" (2 Corinthians 1:6). Note he wasn't saying that his suffering is making the Corinthian believers just before God. Rather, he was saying that his suffering made him able to be "equipped to administer divine encouragement to them when they were afflicted and to ensure their preservation and spiritual well-being when they underwent trial."[7] This is shown by Paul's statement that he knew "that as you are partakers of the sufferings, so also you will partake of the consolation" (1:7). His suffering and consolation proved that the Corinthians' suffering would also be comforted.

Paul also explained what the suffering is. In verses 8 through 11 he described "trouble" that came to him in Asia, a "sentence of death." But he praised God that they were delivered from death, and said that through prayer, the Corinthians helped Paul and his companions.

So we see that the suffering Paul endured was for the benefit of the Corinthians, but that also the Corinthians participated in Paul's suffering and consolation. We also see that Paul assumed suffering on behalf of Christ, or suffering in the name of Christ will happen—not just to him, but to all Christians.

In light of this teaching, Colossians 1:24 becomes clearer: "I now rejoice in my sufferings for you, and fill up in my flesh what is lacking in the afflictions of Christ, for the sake of His body, which is the church." There are two ideas expressed in this verse: suffering for Christ, and suffering on behalf of Christ for others.

We're going to transition now from the more general and commonly understood statement that Christians suffer *for* Christ to the more particular and less understood concept that Christian suffering can be partaking of, and can even be a completing of, the afflictions *of* Christ. We want to declare up front that such a proposition is *not* asserting that anything other or more than the work of Christ on the cross is redemptive. Christ has *already* made the full payment for sin. But as we will later explain, our suffering for Christ may involve our *application* of the benefits of that price to others—that price *only Christ paid*. In our opinion, Paul was teaching that to the extent our suffering is done in connection with our applying to the church or the world the gracious effects of Christ's redemptive act, we are participating in the afflictions of Christ. The reason for Paul's discriminate use of "afflictions" and "sufferings" in Colossians 1:24 will later be revealed. Let's begin by contrasting what is meant by "participating in Christ's sufferings" with allusions to two theological systems.

Biblical Examples of Suffering with Christ

Paul's Own Suffering

The apostle Paul is the quintessential example of suffering. His humble attitude and endurance serves as a model for us. Paul suffered both for Christ's name and for others.

1. *Acts 9:16*—"I will show him how many things he must suffer for My name's sake." The suffering of Paul alluded to here is an effect of the evangelistic activity God planned for the apostle as stated in 9:15. It therefore is a summary of Acts 13–28 as indicated by the following three texts, as well as a theme frequently found in the apostle's letters.

   > *Acts 14:19*—"They stoned Paul and dragged him out of the city, supposing him to be dead."

   > *Acts 16:23*—"When they had laid many stripes on them, they threw them into prison."

   > *Acts 24:21*—"Concerning the resurrection of the dead I am being judged by you this day."

2. *Romans 9:2*—"I have great sorrow and continual grief in my heart." Suffering for Christ may be in mind and soul, not just in body. Paul's sorrow was for unsaved Israel. We suffer in our concerns for others, too, as a later text reveals.

3. *1 Corinthians 4:11*—"To the present hour we both hunger and thirst, and we are poorly clothed, and beaten, and homeless."

Why were Paul and his fellow missionaries homeless, poorly clothed, hungry, and thirty? Is it because they were too lazy to work? No, it was because, while sometimes working, in general, their ministry endeavors were so demanding and time consuming they had no opportunity to be regularly employed.

This is our occasion to look at how we spend our time and energy. The time that we are able to give to serve Christ and how much energy we have to do this work may vary. Many of us, particularly younger people and young working adults, have leftover time and energy to serve in some ministry, if we will prioritize their time. All too quickly, hours become weeks and weeks become years, but each minute is precious and useful for serving. Let's not allow our time to be wasted. Are there not scores of needs in every one of our churches or in parachurch—even small needs—that we can meet for the cause of Christ?

Consider a dear elderly saint who was noted for her loving greeting and caring hug to others in her church foyer each Sunday. She was often seen in the church office folding bulletins, and she cooked and invited the adult Sunday school class she attended to her home. These are but a few ways she served the church and our Lord. That she served in "small ways" doesn't mean her efforts were insignificant. Someday in heaven, her reward will be just as great as that given to those who served in more obvious ways.

4. *2 Corinthians 11:23-28*—Paul lists his credentials as a servant of Christ: "...far more imprisonments, beaten

times without number, often in danger of death. Five times I received from the Jews thirty-nine lashes. Three times I was beaten with rods, once I was stoned, three times I was in shipwreck...dangers from rivers, dangers from robbers, dangers from my countrymen, dangers from the Gentiles, dangers in the city, dangers in the wilderness, dangers on the sea, dangers among false brethren...labor and hardship through many sleepless nights, in hunger and thirst, often without food, in cold and exposure...the daily pressure upon me of concern for all the churches" (NASB).

Note that phrase "the daily pressure upon me of concern for all the churches." Clearly, even were Paul *not* lashed or stoned or hungry or homeless, because of his concern for the church, he still suffered for Christ. Because of that concern, the apostle spent much time in prayer for other Christians and for the churches (Ephesians 1:16; Philippians 1:4; 1 Thessalonians 1:2; Philemon 4). For us to be willing to help other Christians in spite of hardships that may come to us is to act like the apostle Paul and fill up the afflictions of Christ.

5. *2 Corinthians 12:15*—"I will very gladly spend and be spent for your souls." Paul gave his life every day for the needs of others. Is this not the mind of Christ, who died not for Himself but for others? His identification with the denial of Jesus is also seen in Galatians 2:20: "I have been crucified with Christ."

This is what enabled the apostle's marvelously efficient ministry. He counted himself dead so that he could live without the restraint of personal ambitions inhibiting his service or calling to serve Christ.

6. *1 Corinthians 15:31*—"I die daily."

Let's review: Scripture seems to indicate that we may suffer for or with Christ in a variety of ways and to different extents. It was promised to Paul that suffering would come, and he gladly accepted this call both for Christ and on behalf of the church. His example of suffering should be a guide to us.

The Suffering of Epaphroditus

Perhaps one of the greatest examples of self-sacrifice on behalf of others is a little-known saint named Epaphroditus. He is named only twice in the New Testament, both times in Paul's letter to the Philippians. Paul calls Epaphroditus his "brother, fellow worker, and fellow soldier" and "the one who ministered to my need" (Philippians 2:25). Apparently Epaphroditus was quite sick—Paul wrote: "He was sick almost unto death; but God had mercy on him, and not only on him but on me also, lest I should have sorrow upon sorrow" (verse 27).

Clearly Paul had a special place in his heart for Epaphroditus. The latter's death would have caused Paul even more sorrow on top of what he already was enduring as a result of his Roman imprisonment. We don't know much about Epaphroditus's life, but we do know a little about his character. Instead of bemoaning his situation, Epaphroditus was concerned for the Philippians. He was distressed that the Philippians were worried about his sickness. Paul went on to say, "He came close to death, not regarding his life, to supply what was lacking in your service toward me" (Philippians 2:30).

Apparently Epaphroditus was so committed to serving Paul that he disregarded his own welfare. The Greek phrase translated "not regarding his life" is probably too timid. The term has the meaning of brashly exposing one's self to danger, or boldly risking one's life. Epaphroditus risked his life serving Paul. Here was someone ready to give his life for Christ in the service of others, and he can serve as an inspiration to all of us.

We could argue that because Paul was an apostle, we cannot relate to him in our service for Christ. Paul was supernaturally energized to endure great suffering, we might say. But in Epaphroditus, our excuses are destroyed. Here is someone who, to our knowledge, was just like us. He isn't an apostle; he was a committed Christian willing to give his life to serve.

Christian Suffering for Christ

1. *Luke 9:23*—"If anyone wishes to come after Me, let him deny himself, and take up his cross *daily*, and follow Me" (emphasis added). Jesus promised that following Him would mean suffering. There are some who say that the committed, faithful, Christian will be blessed physically and mentally—so much so that a lack of money or a serious illness is evidence of a lack of enough faith. But even a cursory glance at Jesus' teachings, and the examples of Paul and Epaphroditus, show this is not so. Yes, Christians will know blessings, but they will also know affliction.

   We agree with Norval Geldenhuys's conclusion that our Lord's call to follow Him is *not* referencing common human problems such as diseases or disappointments. Rather, this call has reference to "the things which have to be suffered and lost in the service of Christ..."[8]

   Luke 9:23 expressly states that if we desire to follow Christ, then we must deny ourselves. We must put the service of Christ before the service of self. And this must be done not merely on the basis of a one-time commitment to Christ, but daily. Again, in 1 Corinthians 15:31, Paul exclaimed, "I die daily." Every day we must deny ourselves and pick up our cross and do whatever it takes for us to do the will of God. And when we do so, we must pray for God's enabling grace.

2. *John 15:20-21*—"Remember...if they persecuted Me, they will also persecute you...all these things they will do to you for My name's sake." While these words were spoken to the remaining 11 disciples, they apply to Christians in every age. The safe conditions in which many of

us profess our faith may lull us into a state of untested commitment to Christ. This may be disadvantageous to us, for faith can be proven by trials (1 Peter 1:7).

Perhaps it is wise for those of us who live in environments of security, peace, and prosperity to practice the mental discipline of testing our own faith by honestly making assessments of what we would willingly do and give up for Christ were it made clear that such self-denials were God's will for us. You may be aware that in the imperial persecutions of Christians in the early church, those persecuted could escape their terrible tortures if only they would recant their faith and vocally embrace the Roman gods, including the emperor. Have we become such soft Christians that we would deny Christ in such testings, or are we determined to do God's will regardless of the cost?

3. *Acts 7:57-58*—"They cried out with a loud voice, stopped their ears, and ran at him with one accord; and they cast him out of the city and stoned him." Stephen paid a high price for speaking divinely revealed truth: the risen Christ is "in charge." Christ, the resurrected One, is at the place of power at the right hand of God. And that's still true today. Does that reality stir us and motivate us? Are we hungry to experience the "power of His resurrection" (Philippians 3:10)? Pray that your service to God becomes much more than just going to church on Sunday. Few, if any of us, incur suffering just by going to church.

4. *Romans 8:17*—"...if indeed we suffer with Him..." If? We are heirs *if* we suffer? Now that is a troubling statement! Yet, the "if" (Greek, *ei)* is there. Bible commentator Douglas Moo understands Paul to mean that the Christian's glorious inheritance is attained only through suffering. "We must follow Christ's road to glory, and

He first suffered before glorification."[9] So must we literally, physically die on a cross to be glorified?

The notion that we all may suffer in different ways and to different degrees must be accepted. The principle of *considering* ourselves crucified with Christ (Romans 6:4; Galatians 2:20; 1 Corinthians 15:31) is applicable here. How may a person sit comfortably at a desk or dinner table and know inner suffering associated with the determination to deny himself of anything displeasing to God? For example, isn't resolving to quit the habit of alcohol or drugs a form of suffering? So, in the same manner, isn't a resolve to deny self and serve and obey Christ a form of suffering? We think so.

5. *1 Thessalonians 2:14*—"You also suffered the same things…" This text mentions a suffering by "the churches of God," suggesting that suffering as a Christian was commonplace in that time. We all know of places or occasions where the persecution of Christians occurs even today.

6. *2 Timothy 1:8; 2:3*—"Share with me in the sufferings for the gospel…endure hardship as a good soldier of Jesus Christ." Paul likely wrote 2 Timothy during his second imprisonment, soon before his death by the Romans. He said he was suffering for the gospel. Paul encouraged Timothy, who was not imprisoned, to join him in that suffering. In 2 Timothy 1:8, the phrase "suffering with" is a Greek verb made of three parts: *patheo* ("suffer") *kakos* ("bad") *syn* ("together"). It essentially means experiencing bad treatment as a consequence of doing gospel work. Undergoing personal loss for ministering to others is suffering for the gospel, and that is equivalent to suffering with Christ.

7. *1 Peter 2:21*—"You have been called for this purpose, since Christ also suffered for you, leaving you an example

for you to follow in His steps" (NASB). Isn't this remarkable? We are actually called to suffer!

8. *1 Peter 4:13*—"To the degree that you share the sufferings of Christ, keep on rejoicing" (NASB).

Here it is stated explicitly that we may "share the sufferings of Christ." This cannot mean only to actually die for
Christ because (1) *katho* ("to the degree") suggests that
this suffering occurs at various levels, and (2) verses 14-16
confirm there are a variety of ways this suffering can
occur. So, sharing in the suffering of Christ may occur
in varied ways as a result of giving to the needy, cleaning
the church building, fasting and prayer for others, study-
ing hard for teaching a Sunday school lesson, or being
belittled for our faith by others. It might be something
as small as being the object of the giggling of members
of a discussion forum when you say you believe God
created the universe.

9. *1 Peter 5:9-10*—"...the same experiences of suffering
are being accomplished by your brethren who are in the
world. And after you have suffered for a little while, the
God of all grace, who called you to His eternal glory
in Christ, will Himself perfect, confirm, strengthen,
and establish you" (NASB). Here again is the sequence in
Christian experience: suffering, glorification.

From Suffering to Glorification

Does the Christian participate in the suffering of Christ? We have
seen that Christians are promised suffering. We suffer for Christ and
for others on Christ's behalf. In this sense, we suffer with Christ.

Christ promised we would suffer because of Him. Paul suffered on
Christ's behalf by preaching the gospel and serving others. Epaphroditus suffered sickness near to the point of death while serving Paul.
Over and over again in the New Testament Epistles, Christians are
reminded they will suffer for Christ. And there is no doubt that we

suffer with Christ—we as the church are "the body of Christ" (Colossians 1:24). When the church suffers, Christ suffers.

Moreover, Christ suffered because of His message and on our behalf on the cross. So we too suffer for His message, and on behalf of others by sacrificing for each other. In this way we participate in Christ's suffering, and He in ours.

But that isn't the end of the story. We are also promised comfort, consolation, and eventually glorification. The Christian has this glorious hope as he bears the burden of suffering with Christ.

Chapter Nine

Does Prayer Change the Mind of God?

How often have we been asked to pray for someone who is in the midst of suffering? Beyond an expression of compassion and empathy, what role does prayer play? What should we do when someone asks us for prayer, and what should we expect when we ask others to pray for us? And one of the more difficult questions along these lines is this: Does prayer change God's mind? We know the Bible tells us to pray, but why, and how?

An interesting story is told in 1 Kings 18—an account of a contest between the false god of the northern Israelites and the God of Abraham, Isaac, and Jacob. Who was truly God—Baal, or Yahweh? As the prophets of Baal pleaded to their god, there was no response:

> They took the bull that was given them, and they prepared it and called upon the name of Baal from morning until noon, saying, "O Baal, answer us!" But there was no voice, and no one answered. And they limped around the altar that they had made. And at noon Elijah mocked them, saying, "Cry aloud, for he is a god. Either he is musing, or he is relieving himself, or he is on a journey, or perhaps he is asleep and must be awakened" (1 Kings 18:26-27 ESV).

No matter how much the prophets of Baal prayed, leaped around, and even cut their own bodies (verse 28), the expectation of help from this god was nil, for he was not the living God. Elijah urged the prophets of Baal to yell louder to Baal because he might be deep in thought (musing), or he might be relieving himself and thus could not be disturbed, or perhaps he was on a journey and inaccessible, or maybe he was sound asleep and would need to be awakened.

All of these human attributes are given to Baal by the prophet Elijah, traits that reflected in no way the living and infinite God of Israel. The one who is always with His people, who neither slumbers nor sleeps, who is all-knowing and unlimited, answered in a spectacular manner (18:38) to Elijah's simple and brief prayer (18:36-37) to come to the aid of the covenant people to bring them back to Himself (18:39).

The true God can be relied upon to measure up to His attributes and fulfill His promises to His people. We need to rely upon the promises that truly belong to us (not claiming those made to others in Scripture), because God will always work for our benefit and His glory.

By Way of Reminder

Though we surveyed God's attributes earlier in this book, we are going to briefly review them here because a right knowledge of His key attributes will help us avoid falling into common misconceptions about prayer.

Omniscient

God is all-knowing. He knows all things in eternity (Isaiah 46:9-10) and nothing is hidden from His sight (Hebrews 4:13). Nothing comes as a surprise to Him, and He does not learn things as time goes by.

Omnipotent

God is all-powerful. He created and controls all things, and there is nothing outside of His control (Job 38–40). Nothing happens that He did not either direct or allow, and nothing has power over Him.

Immutable

God does not change. Because He is omniscient and perfect, He does not change His mind. He does not change His plans or decisions (Malachi 3:6).

Perfect

God is perfect. He does not make oversights, errors, miscalculations, or any other mistakes. To do so would violate His omniscience, omnipotence, and immutability. Every decision or action on God's part is perfect.

Impassible

Things in creation do not affect God. As we saw in chapters 5 and 6, this does not mean God does not empathize with our suffering. It simply means He is not forced into doing something on account of our suffering. Nor does it mean He will change His decision or plan because of what is happening to us. He cares for us from all eternity.

What Prayer Is Not

There are many misconceptions about prayer, sometimes made by well-meaning and sincere people who may simply have not studied carefully what the Bible says. They may come upon a passage and take it out of context and thus come to a wrong understanding, or they have been misinformed by unbiblical teaching regarding prayer.

Prayer Does Not Inform God

God knows in eternity everything that has ever and will ever happen here on earth. To God, all of history is in the present. Because God knows all things, He does not need our prayers to inform Him of what is taking place. Despite popular (albeit non-Christian) media portrayals to the contrary, God's dwelling place is not some cosmic call-center, waiting for your message to come in so God can send an angel to help take care of whatever problem you might be experiencing. If God needed your input, He would not be all-knowing, all powerful, or perfect.

We may be tempted to think that God is too busy to notice us when we are in times of distress. After all, He's busy upholding the universe, right? However, the Bible says God *does* know our needs. Jesus tells us that God doesn't even forget a single sparrow, and we are "of more value than many sparrows" (Luke 12:7). As we will see in a moment, Jesus taught that God already knows what we need before we even ask.

Prayer Does Not Force God's Hand

When I (Wayne) was a boy, I was told a story about prayer being a way to make God do our bidding. Two men were flying in a small plane when the weather became stormy. There was a heavy downpour, and lightning crashing all around them. The pilot said, "God, now stop all this foolishness, we've got to get to our destination." As if supernaturally, the clouds cleared and they were able to continue their flight safely. It takes great arrogance to think we can tell God what to do, and to think we can address the Creator and Sustainer of the universe so flippantly. We are not in a poker game with God, strategizing how we can "call" God and force His hand.

We cannot use prayer to force God to act and give us what we want. There are some who say that through prayer, whatever we want will be given to us. If we want to be free from pain and suffering, we should simply pray for them to go away, and God has no choice but to do it. If we want health and prosperity, it is our right, so God must give us what we ask for.

But the Bible says, it is the Lord who directs and controls, not us. The apostle James warns, "Come now, you who say, 'Today or tomorrow we will go into such and such a town and spend a year there and trade and make a profit'—yet you do not know what tomorrow will bring. What is your life? For you are a mist that appears for a little time and then vanishes" (James 4:13 ESV). James reminds us that our earthly life is but a moment in length, and we do not know when it will end. He continues, "Instead you ought to say, 'If the Lord wills, we will live and do this or that'" (James 4:15 ESV). To those who say it is wrong to pray that things would be done in the Lord's will, James answers, "As it is, you boast in your arrogance. All such boasting is evil" (James 4:16 ESV).

There was a woman who belonged to a group that teaches those who pray for deliverance from sickness will be healed—that is, if they have enough faith. In time, she was afflicted with cancer. The pastor assured her and her family that she would be healed. All they needed to do was pray. And so they prayed. Yet she got worse and worse. The church members prayed that God would deliver her from her sickness, as He "promised to do." In essence, they thought their prayers would force God to heal her. Eventually she succumbed to the cancer and died. The family was torn apart. How could this be? Because God keeps His promises, did she die because she didn't have enough faith? Or because the family and the congregation didn't have enough faith?

Instead of seeing the error of their thinking—that perhaps it was God's plan to take the woman home, or that she might glorify Him through her suffering—they thought the problem was a lack of faith. But prayer is not a means of forcing God into action, or manipulating Him for our benefit.

Prayer Is Not to Give God a Better Plan

OUR PLAN OR GOD'S PLAN?

Sometimes when we try to get out of a difficult situation, God has a different plan. So no matter how hard we try, our attempts to escape just never seems to work. So we pray, "God, if you would just allow me to do what I think is best, things would work out!"

There was a man who was discontent with his life. His wife did not respect the job he had. She thought he was not achieving his potential, and not providing enough for the family. He prayed for "contentment" with his job, asking God to show him if he was supposed to remain at this job or move on. Because he never became content, he assumed God was telling him to go somewhere else. He conceived all kinds of excuses why his current job was "not God's plan" for his life. He began to think about how to change his circumstances by finding a "better job." But every time he thought he had a lead on a potential career, things would fall apart. He tried applying for all kinds of jobs, and each time he wound up at a dead end. Through this whole process he prayed that God would open a door to an opportunity for a better life.

This pursuit went on for several years. All the while, the man was trying to go after "a better plan" than God's, thinking each job he tried for was the right plan when, in reality, he was imposing his own desires on God. Eventually he realized that the job he had left long ago had given him the flexibility to spend time with his family and had been an encouraging Christian workplace. While it didn't pay what his wife thought he should be making, the job had provided for the family's needs and was a place where he could discuss the Bible and share his spiritual struggles with others. In the end, he realized that what he thought was a better plan for his life was in fact the wrong plan the whole time.

A Godly Man Falls

Another man, an otherwise godly man, also thought he had a better plan than God. His name was Josiah, and he was the king of Judah (the southern kingdom of Israel). Josiah was a godly king—he cleansed Judah of idolatry and resumed proper worship of God. But after doing all this in obedience to God, he made a baffling decision. Josiah heard that the Pharaoh Necho and his army were passing through Judah on their way to help the Assyrians. Perhaps thinking he would hinder the Assyrians (as the old proverb goes, the friend of my enemy is also my enemy), Josiah marched to meet Necho. Necho sent messengers to Josiah, saying, "What have I to do with you, king of Judah? I have not come against you this day, but against the house with which I have war; for God commanded me to make haste. Refrain from meddling with God, who is with me, lest He destroy you" (2 Chronicles 35:21).

Josiah "did not heed the words of Necho from the mouth of God" (verse 22). He thought his plan was better, so he attacked the Egyptians. Unfortunately, Josiah was shot with an arrow and died a short time later. While there is no indication in the text that Josiah prayed about what to do, it is clear that he ignored the Lord's will and followed his own plan.

How often do we do the same, but go even further, praying our own plan to God and thinking it is from Him? How often do we allow our own desires (good-intentioned or not) to cloud our vision? This is not the proper use of prayer.

Prayer Is Not to Change God's Mind

As we've said earlier, God does not change. Therefore, prayer cannot be used to alter God's decisions or actions. However, there are some who disagree with that. They see prayer as being more powerful than God's will—so powerful, in fact, that God is subject to our prayers. They argue that the Bible gives examples of people who changed God's mind through their prayers. For example, they point to 2 Kings 20:1-6. This passage is especially relevant because it deals with a person who was suffering. King Hezekiah was "sick and was at the point of death" (verse 1). The prophet Isaiah came to him and gave him this sobering news: "Set your house in order, for you shall die; you shall not recover" (verse 1 ESV). When Hezekiah heard this, he prayed, "Now, O LORD, please remember how I have walked before you in faithfulness and with a whole heart, and have done what is good in your sight" (verse 3). Then he "wept bitterly."

Unexpectedly, as Isaiah is leaving, God turns him around and gives him these words for Hezekiah:

> I have heard your prayer; I have seen your tears. Behold, I will heal you. On the third day you shall go up to the house of the LORD, and I will add fifteen years to your life. I will deliver you and this city out of the hand of the king of Assyria, and I will defend this city for my own sake and for my servant David's sake (2 Kings 20:5-6 ESV).

At first glance, and without context, we might think that God changed His mind about Hezekiah. But is that what really happened? There is a parallel account of this event in 2 Chronicles that sheds light on the situation. Previous to Hezekiah becoming sick, the mighty Assyrian army laying siege to Jerusalem had been singlehandedly defeated—not through Israel's military force, but through divine intervention. The people rejoiced and brought gifts to the Lord. They also brought gifts to Hezekiah, and Hezekiah was "exalted in the sight of all nations" (2 Chronicles 32:23). There is no indication that Hezekiah refused these gifts or the adoration. We can gain further insight about this from Isaiah, who recorded this response from Hezekiah:

> O Lord, by these things men live, and in all these is the life of my spirit. Oh restore me to health and make me live! Behold, it was for my welfare that I had great bitterness; but in love you have delivered my life from the pit of destruction, for you have cast all my sins behind your back (Isaiah 38:16-17 ESV).

Hezekiah's sickness, it seems, wasn't a random event. Also, it seems God's plan all along was for Hezekiah to repent of his arrogant attitude. The Lord's granting of Hezekiah's prayer request isn't a matter of Hezekiah forcing God to change His plans. Rather, it is God acknowledging Hezekiah's repentant heart. When God told Hezekiah he would die, He wasn't stating a promise or a prophecy, but a warning. God didn't change His mind; rather, He reacted to Hezekiah's change of heart. Hezekiah would die if something did not change.

It is difficult to comprehend how God, being infinite, operates in a finite world. God works in ways that, from our human perspective, seem to sometimes contradict His nature. But the *method* He uses to interact with us should not be taken to mean God has finite attributes.

Unfortunately, Hezekiah's repentance was short-lived. When envoys from Babylon heard of his sickness and miraculous recovery, God left Hezekiah to his own devices "in order to test him and to

know all that was in his heart" (2 Chronicles 32:31). Instead of praising God and giving Him the credit, Hezekiah showed the envoys all
his wealth. It is at this point God gave a promise that was eventually
fulfilled. The Lord promised that this wealth would all be carried off
to Babylon, and that some of Hezekiah's sons would be taken away
to become eunuchs in service to the Babylonian king. Even after this
dire prediction, Hezekiah's arrogance did not abate. He flippantly
answered, "Why not, if there will be peace and security in my days?"
(2 Kings 20:19 esv). This time there was no change of heart on Hezekiah's part, and God's promise came to fruition.

What Prayer Is

Prayer is our means of communicating with God. Though God
does not need our prayers, He does desire fellowship with us. He could
act without us ever being involved, but He does not. Through prayer
we seek His forgiveness. Through prayer we worship Him. Through
prayer we give Him thanks. Through prayer we ask Him to meet our
needs. While our prayers do not affect God—that is, they do not alter
His infinite attributes, such as His wisdom, goodness, and holiness—
we definitely are affected by our prayers. We benefit from our prayers
in several ways. Moreover, *God has chosen to work through prayer to
accomplish His will.* And ultimately, we glorify God through prayer.

Prayer Is for Our Benefit

We Can Learn Through Prayer

As Christians we are called to study God's Word as well as meditate
on it. Joshua 1:8 says, "This Book of the Law shall not depart from
your mouth, but you shall meditate in it day and night, that you may
observe to do according to all that is written in it." It is important at
this point to clarify what is meant here by the word "meditate." Rather
than the Eastern religious idea of *clearing one's mind* of thoughts, biblical meditation is the *filling of one's mind* with thoughts about the Word.
It is contemplating on His message and reflecting on God's actions
and what the passage may teach us about His ways.

As we study, we can meditate in the form of prayer. We can ask, "God, what does this passage call me to do?" or "What is Your message here?" As we study the Word, we should let it permeate our thinking so that our thoughts are always centered upon it. Psalm 1:2 says "blessed is the man" whose "delight is in the law of the LORD, and in His law he meditates day and night."

One cannot but help pray while contemplating the Psalms, as well as the many hymns of praise and thanksgiving throughout the Bible. These songs and poems teach us the character and activities of God. Simply by meditating on Moses' song in Exodus 15 we learn that God is all-powerful, merciful, holy, and will reign forever. Mary's song in Luke 1 tells us God is our Savior, He is just, He provides for the needy, and He keeps His promises. Biblical meditation can help you to be "transformed by the renewing of your mind, that you may prove what is that good and acceptable and perfect will of God" (Romans 12:2).

WE CAN BE COMFORTED BY PRAYER

During times of suffering, prayer can be a great comfort. Psalm 119:76 says,

> Let, I pray, Your merciful kindness be for my comfort, according to Your word to Your servant. Let Your tender mercies come to me, that I may live; for Your law is my delight.

If we continually meditate on God's Word, we will be comforted. And others are comforted when they know we are praying for them in their time of distress. Sometimes simply knowing that others care enough to pray for us during a time of need is a great comfort. And it's reassuring to remember that God is "the Father of mercies and God of all comfort" (2 Corinthians 1:3). David, feeling despair, reminds himself,

> Why are you cast down, O my soul? And why are you disquieted within me? Hope in God; for I shall yet praise

Him, the help of my countenance and my God (Psalm
42:11).

The apostle Paul prayed for the comfort of the Thessalonians in
2 Thessalonians 2:16-17: "Now may our Lord Jesus Christ Himself,
and our God and Father, who has loved us and given us everlasting
consolation and good hope by grace, comfort your hearts and establish
you in every good word and work." The Greek word translated "comfort" means "to relieve someone from sorrow or distress." In this way
Paul prays that God would keep their hearts from sorrow.

Prayer Is a Means to an End

One of the ways God has chosen to interact with His people is
through prayer. We will see this in a moment in the prayers of Elijah.
Sometimes *God uses our prayers as a means to an end.* It isn't that God
cannot act until we pray, or doesn't know the end that is achieved
through prayer. God can choose to act regardless of us. He can miraculously heal someone without anyone praying for that person. He can
accomplish His will even if no one prays that His will be done. He
can give us things without us asking for them. But God, the infinite Creator and Lord of the universe, has chosen to act through our
prayers.

Rather than us controlling God through prayer, prayer is our way
of interacting with God. The apostle James taught that if anyone lacks
wisdom, "let him ask of God, who gives to all liberally and without
reproach, and it will be given to him" (James 1:5). But those who
ask should believe they will receive it, without doubting, "for he who
doubts is like a wave of the sea driven and tossed by the wind. For let
not that man suppose that he will receive anything from the Lord; he
is a double-minded man, unstable in all his ways" (1:6-8).

Is God forced to give us wisdom when we ask for it? No, certainly
not. But here we see that God has chosen to work through prayer
to provide us with something beneficial, something He wants us to
have—wisdom for dealing with the trials of life.

Prayer Is a Way to Glorify God

How many of the psalms are prayers of exaltation to the Lord? Because prayer is a direct conversation we have with God, prayer is a wonderful way to worship God. David prays, "I will praise You, O Lord my God, with all my heart, and I will glorify Your name forevermore. For great is Your mercy toward me, and You have delivered my soul from the depths of Sheol" (Psalm 86:12-13).

We can pray thanksgiving to God for all that He does, as David did. We find another example of this in Psalm 30, where David recounted all the things God had done for him, thanking and praising Him for them. We are told that this psalm was recited at the dedication of David's house in Jerusalem. For the first time as Israel's leader, David had a place to call home. He had been constantly on the run from Saul, often living in the desert. Now he had a refuge, and was safe in his palace. David thanked God for lifting him up in his troubled times (verse 1). He recounted how he had cried out to God, and God had answered him (verse 2). God had turned David's mourning over his circumstances into "dancing" (verse 11). David concludes with these words: "To the end that my glory may sing praise to You and not be silent. O Lord my God, I will give thanks to You forever" (verse 12).

Examples of Prayer in the Bible

There are hundreds of examples of prayer in the Bible. We will look at some of the prayers of Abraham, Elijah, and Jesus as examples to give us an idea of how we can communicate with God.

Abraham

The story of Abraham's conversation with God concerning Sodom and Gomorrah is a very interesting account of how God can interact with His people. Some see Abraham as trying to trick God into not destroying the evil cities, but a careful study shows that isn't the case. The story takes place as God and Abraham look over the cities of Sodom and Gomorrah. God reveals to Abraham that the sins of the cities were very great. The two "men" (angels) who were with God go down to "see whether they have done altogether according to the outcry against it" (Genesis 18:21). Abraham, knowing how God deals with sinful people, and knowing that Lot, his nephew, and his family were there, asks God,

> Would You also destroy the righteous with the wicked? Suppose there were fifty righteous within the city; would You also destroy the place and not spare it for the fifty righteous that were in it? Far be it from You to do such a thing as this, to slay the righteous with the wicked, so that the righteous should be as the wicked; far be it from You! Shall not the Judge of all the earth do right? (Genesis 18:23-25).

God answers, "If I find in Sodom fifty righteous within the city, then I will spare all the place for their sakes" (verse 26). Abraham, hedging his bet possibly because he knew there weren't even 50 righteous people in the cities, asks if God would destroy the cities if even 45 righteous were found. Again, God replies that He would relent if even 45 were found. And so it goes until Abraham gets down to ten. God says that He would relent even for the sake of ten people.

Now some people think that God would have had to change his decision to destroy the cities if ten righteous people could have been found, which, of course, is moot, because in Sodom there were only four. They argue that if God had ultimately decided to destroy the city knowing there were not even ten, then there is no reason why God should have strung Abraham along. Why didn't God simply tell Abraham, "Look, I know you are going to ask for mercy down to ten people because your nephew lives there, so let's cut to the chase. I'll spare Lot, his wife, and his daughters from the destruction I will bring upon the city, no matter what you ask."

Fortunately for humanity, God has not chosen to operate this way. Instead, He has chosen to interact with us, to have fellowship with us. As a result, sometimes from our perspective it seems God changes His mind. In this case, our perception is that God was going to destroy the city. Abraham intervened, and God decided that if there were only 50 righteous people in the city he wouldn't destroy it, and so on. Notice Abraham's wording, however. This exchange took place in a hypothetical realm. Abraham asked, "Suppose there were fifty…" and God, knowing there weren't 50 righteous people, answered, "If there are fifty I will relent." There is no reason to believe God was changing His plans every time Abraham lowered the number. At the heart of the conversation, God was conveying to Abraham that He must deal justly with sin, but at the same time, He will show mercy on behalf of the righteous.

The fact is, God, in eternity past, knew Sodom and Gomorrah would become utterly sinful and decided to destroy the cities. However, He also knew Lot and his family would be there, and He had a plan in place to save them from the destruction. Finally, God knew Abraham was motivated by compassion for his nephew and was not challenging His authority by asking the questions. God interacted with Abraham in an anthropomorphic manner. In the communication, God displayed human-like characteristics for our benefit. It is one way the Infinite Being has chosen to interact with finite beings.

Elijah

The prophet Elijah had one of the toughest jobs in the entire Bible. As one of the last prophets of God in Israel, after all others had turned to Baal worship, he was forced into exile. We will look at two of his prayers and how they apply to suffering.

THE WIDOW AND HER SON

While Elijah was in exile, he stayed with a widow and her son. God had miraculously provided for the three of them, supplying enough flour and oil during a severe famine caused by the drought God had sent upon the land. Then tragedy struck. We read in 1 Kings 17:17, "Now it happened after these things that the son of the woman who owned the house became sick. And his sickness was so serious that there was no breath left in him." The widow's husband had already died, and now she was about to lose her son. As is often the case, she looked for an explanation for what was happening, and as is often the case, fear and suffering led to anger: "She said to Elijah, 'What have I to do with you, O man of God? Have you come to me to bring my sin to remembrance, and to kill my son?'" (verse 18). In her flawed logic, the woman failed to acknowledge that God had saved her and her son from famine, and she blamed the prophet's presence for the imminent death of her son.

Elijah, who was deeply moved by all this suffering, carried the son to his bedroom and cried out to God, "O LORD my God, have You also brought tragedy on the widow with whom I lodge, by killing her son?" (verse 20). Elijah then threw himself over the boy and prayed, "O LORD my God, I pray, let this child's soul come back to him" (verse 21). The text says "the LORD heard the voice of Elijah; and the soul of the child came back to him, and he revived" (verse 22). If we left the story right here, we might be led to the conclusions that God (1) needs to be informed of tragic events occurring here on earth, and (2) is moved to action by our prayers. The boy died, Elijah questioned God, then prayed that his life would be returned to him, and the boy was healed.

But we must continue all the way to the end of the story to see the full picture. Elijah carried the boy back downstairs to his mother, who cried, "Now by this I know that you are a man of God, and that the word of the LORD in your mouth is the truth" (verse 24). Here we get a glimpse of how God uses prayer (as well as suffering) to accomplish His purposes. There is no reason to think that God was unaware of the boy's predicament, or that He was moved to action due to Elijah's prayer. Rather, it seems there were some misunderstandings on the part of the widow.

First, she thought the tragedy was caused by her sin, something akin to the proverb "The sins of the father will be visited on the son." Though the Bible does teach that suffering *can* be caused by sin, it does not say that suffering is *always* the result of sin. It is safe to assume that had this been the case, the prophet Elijah would have known about it.

But Elijah's reaction to what happened makes it clear he did not know why this tragedy had struck.

Second, it seems that the widow may have begun to doubt whether Elijah was truly a prophet of God. We don't know how long Elijah had stayed with the widow, but perhaps after a time she, like Israel growing weary of the miraculous manna during its 40-year sojourn in the wilderness, had become complacent. Perhaps by this event she was shocked back to her senses. At any rate, it is clear that God had confirmed to the widow that Elijah was a man of God and that he spoke "the word of the LORD," and this purpose was accomplished partially through Elijah's prayer.

The incident in 1 Kings 17 shows that sometimes prayer can be the means to an end that God wants to accomplish. God wasn't unaware of the widow's predicament regarding her son, and He did not need Elijah to pray before He could act. Rather, God works through our prayer to accomplish His will.

ELIJAH AND THE PROPHETS OF BAAL

When Elijah first proclaimed to Israel that God would send a drought, he said, "As the LORD God of Israel lives, before whom I stand, there shall not be dew nor rain these years, except at my word" (1 Kings 17:1). For three years there was no rain in Israel or the surrounding areas. Then Elijah returned to Israel and confronted the prophets of Baal with a challenge: Who is the God of Israel—Baal, or Yahweh?

In 1 Kings 18 we have the account of this confrontation. Elijah challenged the prophets to get Baal to accept a sacrifice, and even taunted them. All day long the prophets of Baal danced around an altar, and they even cut themselves, trying to get Baal to take a sacrificial offering. At the end of the day, "there was no voice; no one answered, no one paid attention" (verse 29).

Now it was Elijah's turn. He made an altar, prepared the sacrifice, and even poured a lot of water on it. Then he prayed, "Yahweh God of Abraham, Isaac, and Israel, let it be known this day that You are God in Israel and I am Your servant, and that I have done all these things at Your word. Answer me, Yahweh, answer me, that this people may know that You are Yahweh our God, and that You have turned their hearts back to You again" (verses 36-37, personal paraphrase). Immediately fire came down upon the sacrifice, burning it, the wood, the stones, the dirt around the altar, and the water in the trench around the altar. The people of Israel who had been worshipping Baal suddenly had a change of heart. They cried, "Yahweh, He is God! Yahweh, He is God!" (verse 39, personal paraphrase).

Elijah then commanded that the prophets of Baal be seized and promptly executed. When this was done, Elijah went back to the top of Mount Carmel and prayed (the text doesn't say he prayed for rain, but we can assume that's what he was doing). He told his servant to go look for rain clouds. At first, there was nothing. Seven more times Elijah prayed, and finally his servant saw clouds on the horizon. Soon there was a heavy downpour, and the drought was over.

Some see this story as an example of the power prayer can have over God. Because Elijah said rain would not come until *he* commanded it, and it did not rain until Elijah prayed for it, some people assume it was Elijah who was in ultimate control over the rain, and not necessarily God. Even the apostle James *seems* to say this in his letter: "Elijah was a man with a nature like ours, and he prayed earnestly that it would not rain; and it did not rain on the land for three years and six months. And he prayed again, and the heaven gave rain, and the earth produced its fruit" (James 5:17-18).

So was Elijah in control? It may seem so, but we need to recall the promise God made to Israel as they were about to enter into and inherit the Promised Land:

> It shall be that if you earnestly obey My commandments which I command you today, to love the Lord your God and serve Him with all your heart and with all your soul, then I will give you the rain for your land in its season, the early rain and the latter rain, that you may gather in your grain, your new wine, and your oil (Deuteronomy 11:13-14).

Simply put, *obedience* would result in blessing. But there was a warning as well:

> Take heed to yourselves, lest your heart be deceived, and you turn aside and serve other gods and worship them, lest the LORD's anger be aroused against you, and He shut up the heavens so that there be no rain, and the land yield no produce, and you perish quickly from the good land which the LORD is giving you (Deuteronomy 11:16-17).

Israel, in Elijah's time, was doing exactly what God had warned against. He could have simply stopped the rain and waited for Israel to realize their sin. But God, being merciful, used the prophet Elijah to proclaim that a drought was coming. Even three years into the drought, Ahab, king of Israel, failed to realize why there was a drought. When Elijah visited him, Ahab called the prophet a "troubler of Israel." Elijah responded that it was in fact Ahab who had brought trouble on Israel because "you have forsaken the commandments of the LORD and have followed the Baals" (1 Kings 18:18). When the prophets of Baal were defeated and the people returned to worshipping God alone, God fulfilled his promise, and rain came back. God could have simply made the rain return *without* waiting for Elijah's prayers. Yet He chose to operate through human prayers to accomplish His will.

Jesus

It is interesting to note that before almost every major event Jesus was involved in, He prayed. We aren't told what He said, but we can imagine He was making sure His will and the Father's were one. Perhaps He was also asking for the Father's help. Jesus did both of these in the Garden of Gethsemane in John chapter 17, where we are allowed the rare privilege of hearing one of His prayers. We should look to Jesus' example and remember to pray before the important events in our lives.

When it comes to *how* we should pray, Jesus has given us guidelines in what is often called the Lord's Prayer.

THE LORD'S PRAYER

There are two accounts of the Lord's Prayer in the Bible, and the context of each gives us helpful insight about prayer. In Matthew, the prayer appears after the Beatitudes. Jesus taught that we are not to pray hypocritically, making a show of how holy we are. And we are not to use "vain repetitions" (Matthew 6:7). Jesus then went on to say,

> Your Father knows the things you have need of before you ask Him. In this manner, therefore, pray:
>
> Our Father in heaven,
> Hallowed be Your name.
> Your kingdom come.
> Your will be done
> On earth as it is in heaven.
> Give us this day our daily bread.
> And forgive us our debts,
> As we forgive our debtors.
> And do not lead us into temptation,
> But deliver us from the evil one (Matthew 6:8-13).

We see here that prayer ought to acknowledge God, acknowledge our desire for His will, ask Him for our daily provision, ask for forgiveness, and ask for God's help in protecting us from evil. Jesus didn't say to pray *this* prayer every time we pray, but to pray *like this*. When we pray, even during times of suffering, we should keep these principles in mind. Even in the midst of pain, we should acknowledge God's sovereignty. Even in times of need, we should ask God for His provision. When we sin, we should ask for forgiveness. When we experience times of spiritual distress, we should ask for God's protection.

ASKING FOR THE DESIRES OF OUR HEART

Jesus taught that we should live in Him and His words should live in us. If we do this, Jesus promised, "you will ask what you desire, and it shall be done for you" (John 15:7). We are to ask God in prayer for what we desire, and it will be given to us if we are abiding in Him. Jesus said, "By this My Father is glorified, that you bear much fruit; so you will be My disciples" (John 15:8). The more we meditate on God's Word, the more our thoughts are in line with God's. And when our desires are in line with God's, they are given to us. All this is accomplished for God's glory.

PRAYER IN GETHSEMANE

As the culmination of Jesus' earthly ministry drew near, Jesus was fully aware of what He was about to face. He knew He would experience excruciating pain and finally, death. As we study His prayer in the Garden of Gethsemane, we must keep in mind He is not only fully God, but fully man. As a man, He was deeply troubled over what was about to happen. Any of us would be. Luke gives us a glimpse of what was happening:

> [Jesus] was withdrawn from them about a stone's throw, and He knelt down and prayed, saying, "Father, if it is Your will, take this cup away from Me; nevertheless not My will, but Yours, be done." Then an angel appeared to Him from heaven, strengthening Him. And being in agony, He prayed more earnestly. Then His sweat became like great drops of blood falling down to the ground (22:41-44).

In Matthew's account (26:36-46), Jesus prayed, "Let this cup pass from Me" (verse 39). He said this three times, but each time He also asked that the Father's will would be done.

Matthew also recorded Jesus as saying, "My soul is exceedingly sorrowful, even to death" (26:38). Imagine the terror of knowing you are about to die a horrible death. In this moment, Jesus, in his humanity, falters. He asked that "this cup" (the agonizing death He is about to experience) might be taken away. Yet He remained obedient to the Father's will; He did not sin. He continued to acknowledge that He wanted the Father's will to be done, not His (in his humanity). And although He was strengthened by angels, He was still greatly stressed by what He was about to face.

This brings up an important point: When we are suffering, it is not wrong to ask God to end it. If someone is sick or in pain, it is not wrong to pray that the affliction may be taken away. But as Jesus did, we must always acknowledge that it may be God's will for the suffering to continue. Finally, we should not cease praying when the suffering does not end. We should not interpret the continuation of the suffering as a sign that God is not listening, doesn't care, or is unable to help. Sometimes God has a purpose for suffering that we cannot see at the time (or perhaps ever). In the case of Jesus, His suffering was essential to God's plan for our salvation. Without the sacrifice, there would have been no forgiveness of sin. Jesus knew this, so His despair was tempered by being obedient to God's will.

The Holy Spirit, Suffering, and Prayer

The apostle Paul, in his letter to the Romans, wrote,

> The Spirit also helps in our weaknesses. For we do not know what we should pray for as we ought, but the Spirit Himself makes intercession for us with groanings which cannot be uttered. Now He who searches the hearts knows what the mind of the Spirit is, because He makes intercession for the saints according to the will of God (Romans 8:26-27).

The Greek word translated "weakness" here can also mean sickness or infirmity. It is generally used to convey a state of incapacity. We have all felt weak for one reason or another, but we're especially prone to feel weak during times of trouble. We may be in despair over what we should do. Paul gives us wonderful encouragement here, saying that during those times, the Spirit will intercede for us. He knows God's will for us, and will pray accordingly on our behalf. In this way, Paul said, "all things work together for good to those who love God, to those who are the called according to His purpose" (Romans 8:28). Whether we suffer or not, our prayers and the Holy Spirit's intercession on our behalf work together for our good.

The Call to Prayer

As we conclude our look at prayer in the midst of suffering, we need to remember we are called to pray at all times (1 Thessalonians 5:17), not just when we're in pain. Prayer helps us learn and grow closer to God. It turns our focus to Him, and reminds us of who is in charge. And we are to pray not only for our own strength and comfort. We are also to pray for others when they suffer. Sometimes God acts through our prayers, as James said, "The effective, fervent prayer of a righteous man avails much" (James 5:16). Perhaps it is God's will to deliver someone from suffering, and to do so through our prayers. Other times, it is simply a comfort to the one who is suffering to know that others are caring for and thinking about them. Above all, we are called to glorify God, which we can do through prayer, even in the midst of suffering. Clearly, prayer is a very important part of the Christian's life.

Chapter Ten

Being Victorious in the Face of Life's Problems

The Christian life is all about victory. Christ has secured victory over sin and death (1 Corinthians 15:3-4). We are called to be sanctified and victorious over sin in our daily walk (Philippians 2:12-13). We are exhorted to persevere and gain victory over trials and temptations (James 1:12). This life, though filled with pain and suffering, should not cause us to lose sight of the victory that has already been secured by Jesus.

Where Are We?

"Have mercy upon me, O God, according to Your lovingkindness; according to the multitude of Your tender mercies, blot out my transgressions" (Psalm 51:1).

Before we can speak about how to be victorious over sin and suffering, each of us first needs to examine where we are on the road to victory. Let us say at the outset that the efforts that we make on this pathway should not be understood as achievable through human effort alone, but greatly depend on the love and mercy of God, as well as His enablement through the work of the Holy Spirit. We may view ourselves as able to reach up to God, but we should also understand that He is the one who has helped us to do so. As Psalm 113:6-7 says, He has stooped down from the heavens to the earth to lift us out of rubbish heaps. There is no bragging of our accomplishments before God.

God's Special Education

In our public schools the term *special education* refers to the adaptation of learning to accommodate students who have special requirements. Such adaptations vary greatly in their extent according to the student's need or how far the school is required to go to reach the student where he is. It may mean something as simple as the teacher merely limiting the number of words on a spelling test from, say, twenty to ten, or seating the child near the front of the classroom so he can hear better. Or, special education may be quite complex and intensive, to the point of providing a one-on-one teacher's aide, special equipment, and a drastically modified curriculum for a severely or multiply handicapped young person.

Special education is a component of contemporary public education services that are offered to those who have various disabilities. Through these services, students who would otherwise be shut out of the educational system have access to training necessary for them to "make it" in the world. One of the most profound cases of which we are aware is the story of a 13-year-old quadriplegic boy who was only half the normal size and weight of a child his age. He also was speech-impaired and possibly had an intellectual disability.[1] But his intelligence was hard to determine because of the difficulty of testing an individual with such extreme problems.

The school did all it could to meet this boy's needs. An aide was hired just for him. She would wheel him into a classroom for "mainstreaming," where various activities were occurring, and sit next to him in the back of the room. But whatever benefits he gained from that had little to with the teacher's lesson for the rest of the class. It was pure "socializing." Also, as part of her duties, during lunch hour, the aide would remove the boy from his wheelchair and massage and stretch his joints and muscles in an attempt to postpone further dystrophy. The school district provided equipment and instruction to enable the aide to do that.

One year, the parents, specialists, teachers, and aide planned a few learning objectives for this young boy, to perform very simple tasks by most people's standards. One objective was that, by the end of the year, through nearly daily training by the aide, he would be able to navigate by himself his electric wheelchair 25 feet down the hall to another classroom. Another objective was that when the aide lifted him up after he used the toilet, he would shift his tiny body ever so slightly to assist the aide in that lifting. These were his modest goals and school-related learning. Other students his age were busy with algebra, English composition, science, and history, and were improving in basketball, softball, gymnastics, and were planning their dates and dress for the fall dance.

What was particularly special about this young boy was that one day, his teacher distinctly heard him, with much effort due to his speech impediment, say, "I just love Jesus." Has a greater testimony despite length or eloquence ever been given?

Our Need of God

In the spiritual realm, many of us are much like that little boy. We are incapacitated and weak. Why, then, does God desire to come to our aid? What is it about God that causes Him to desire to minister to us in our sin and rebellion? It is not because we are good, or lovable, or beautiful, or especially gifted or skilled. We do not merit God's concern and desire to lift us up to sit us among princes (Psalm 113:8). The reason God does all this is because God is love and not that we are lovable. We, too, can have the touch of God so that "we just love Jesus." We need to understand that every one of us needs "special education" in the spiritual realm.

Not until we know *where we are* and *where we lack* are we able fully to appreciate the great effort that God has made for us—even to the death of Jesus on the cross—and the greatness of the victory that we will experience through Him.

The Roadblocks to Victory

As we walk onward on the path to victory, there can be many obstacles that stand in our way. We'll look at some of them, then look at the assurances God has given us for victory.

Some May Be Sincerely Religious but Wrong

Saul, the learned rabbi, fervent Pharisee, and persecutor of early believers in Jesus was very religious, but also very wrong. Only after meeting the risen Messiah and Savior on the road to the Syrian capital, Damascus, did he begin to embrace the truth of the Jewish Messiah. We see the level of his religious commitment in his own words:

> Circumcised the eighth day, of the nation of Israel, of the tribe of Benjamin, a Hebrew of Hebrews; as to the Law, a Pharisee; as to zeal, a persecutor of the church; as to righteousness which is in the Law, found blameless...I was advancing in Judaism beyond many of my contemporaries, being more extremely zealous for my ancestral traditions (Philippians 3:5-6; Galatians 1:14 NASB).

Saul was religious but wrong! He is determined and yet defiant as he walked north toward Damascus. He was zealous in his efforts to arrest those heretical Jews who asserted that the crucified Jesus is the resurrected Son of God and Messiah. In spite of his considerable training in the Hebrew Scriptures, he had not made the connection between the Old Testament prophecies of the coming Messiah and the man Jesus. This is not surprising, for Jesus Himself said,

> You search the Scriptures because you think that in them you have eternal life; and it is these that testify about Me...if you had believed Moses, you would believe Me; for he wrote of Me...O foolish men and slow of heart to believe in all that the prophets have spoken! Was it not necessary for the Christ to suffer these things and to enter into His glory?" (John 5:39; Luke 24:25-26 NASB).

How ironic that some forms of learning Scripture actually can make one opposed, perhaps unknowingly, to the God of Scripture! So, what should become of Saul? Man's justice might say just let him go on in his blind, self-righteousness way. Let Saul learn only when it is too late for him that he is the chief of sinners (1 Timothy 1:15). Let each mile made toward Damascus sink him further into the mire of error. Let each threat he breathes out against the disciples of Jesus pile higher the hot wrath of God upon him. He deserves the fires of hell!

But God chose to meet Saul where Saul was. It was a meeting arranged by divine grace and not human merit. We don't meet God because we are good, but because God is gracious.

Some May Be Anointed Backsliders

Some of us may be mature or knowledgeable Christians. Some of us serve as pastors, teachers, or in some other church or parachurch office. Some of us love the Word and work hard to understand the depths of it. Some of us have experienced the power of God and have seen His promises fulfilled in our lives. We know His mysteries, and His miracles attest His presence and might to us. His gifts and graces to us are many and wonderful. But none of those things exempt us from testing, do they? Rather, to whom much is given much is required. Neither does a past record of victories over such testing infallibly predict a certain win in every future situation in which we are tempted. Every Christian is vulnerable to backsliding, and the "higher" up we are, the further may be our slide downward.

So it was with David, God's anointed, who, one spring night, was walking on his own roof, from where he "saw a woman bathing; and the woman was very beautiful to behold" (2 Samuel 11:2). Yes, David was kept safe in Jerusalem from the battle against Ammon, but he was in danger nevertheless in a war for the welfare of his soul and his relationship with God. Perhaps that is a clue that some of us are most vulnerable when we are taking a break from God's service?

David was not even safe in his own house. This shows us that temptation can strike us anywhere: in our homes, at our computers, in front of our televisions, at a store, in our churches, at our jobs, or wherever. Yet we have to be in such places! So, the key for us is to turn away at the very first appearance of temptation. And it's also helpful to develop a habit of, all through each day, completely surrendering our hearts and determining to live for the Lord our God and not for ourselves.

So, from his roof, David saw Bathsheba as she bathed and he lusted for her, sinning in his heart before his lust was fulfilled (see Matthew 5:29). That's when David should have realized he had already gone too far. The time to stop looking is before our hearts start lusting.

You probably know that David went on to commit adultery, and had Bathsheba's husband killed. Sin can produce more sin. See how far the mighty can fall? David handled Goliath quite well, but there was a giant growing in his heart that he did not handle so well—his own lust. Trials come both from without and from within. So even were our bodies tucked away in cloisters, our souls are not safe unless our hearts too are set apart for God.

Fortunately for David, the story does not stop there. We also know of David's repentance after his great fall:

> Hide Your face from my sins, and blot out all my iniq-
> uities. Create in me a clean heart, O God, and renew a
> steadfast spirit within me. Do not cast me away from
> Your presence, and do not take Your Holy Spirit from me.
> Restore to me the joy of Your salvation (Psalm 51:9-12).

Some might immediately reject David's repentance and say, "Let David die in his sin. What he did was horrible. There should be a limit to God's benevolence. David had seen enough of God to know not to turn away from Him. David turned his back on God; God should turn His back on David!"

But that is not like our God. God chooses rather to "forgive us our sins and to cleanse us from all unrighteousness" (1 John 1:9). God accepts a broken and a contrite heart (Psalm 51:17). Moreover, He meets us wherever we are, regardless of how far down He must reach. He does so because of His goodness and not ours.

Why not pause now to take a moment to admit to God your unworthiness and thank Him who forgives your transgressions? You can trust Him to receive you because of His loyal love. If you have moved from Him, even if your sin is great, return to Him and trust His grace.

Some May Be Penitents with "Many Sins"

The song "Amazing Grace" has captured the hearts of Christians from the time it was written. The writer, John Newton, had been the captain of a slave ship. He came to faith in Jesus in 1748 and later abandoned his wretched job. The song speaks eloquently of God's grace and forgiveness in spite of our terrible sins with lyrics from 1 Chronicles 17:16-17, where David is amazed at God's choosing of him.[2]

Even if our sins are great, and deep as scarlet, Scripture says we will be made as white as snow. Such is the amazing grace of our God on penitent sinners. One wonderful example of this is found in Luke's Gospel:

> Behold, a woman in the city who was a sinner, when she knew that Jesus was reclining at the table in the Pharisee's house, brought an alabaster flask of fragrant oil, and stood at His feet behind Him weeping; and she began to wash His feet with her tears, and wiped them with the hair of her head; and she kissed His feet and anointed them with the fragrant oil (Luke 7:37-38).

Simon, a Pharisee, had invited our Lord to eat at his home. According to custom, less fortunate people would wait to gather leftovers after such a banquet. A woman who was a sinner, the term used "to identify a person who has a reputation for gross immorality,"[3] came to meet Jesus, possibly as one who was carrying out the aforementioned custom. She also came to minister to Jesus.

Simon was at a loss to understand why Jesus would accept this sinful woman's actions. Simon didn't fully understand Jesus' attitude. His purpose was to save sinners, not to validate self-righteous people like Simon. This woman who had committed many sins was forgiven by the Lord. There is an important lesson for us here: Regardless of the enormity of our guilt, God is willing to love us. Making ourselves better for God is not the answer, making ourselves available to God is.

Some May Be Held Fast in Satan's Grip

Some people, due to the strong grip that Satan has upon their life, find it difficult to free themselves from the evils of this world that bring suffering and disaster into their lives.

How may those bound by evil make themselves available to the deliverance of God? How can they escape destructive practices involving drugs, pornography, and alcohol? Must God wait until the person overcomes the powers of evil and shakes off those shackles on his own? That is impossible to do. We are not able to deliver ourselves. With God's help, we can break free. And no one is beyond hope. Jesus was able to rescue even the Gerasene demonic in Luke 8:26-29.

Nothing is too hard for our God—there is hope! Even where the sturdiest chains of men fail and even where the strongest bindings of Satan hold one prisoner, the Lord our God is not rendered incapable.

Some May Be Unfinished "Miracles"

When it comes to knowing God's power in your life, perhaps you feel as though you are in a rut. You love Christ and want to do great things for God, but find yourself failing to make progress in your Christian walk. Have the struggles of life stalled you in following Christ as you should? It may seem that for every two steps you take forward, you end up taking three steps backward. God can help you. The apostle Peter is a prime example of the way in which God can take a piece of coal to make a diamond. One of the most well-known stories of Scripture is the account in which Peter walked on water to approach Jesus:

> When the disciples saw Him walking on the sea, they were troubled...And Peter answered Him and said, "Lord, if it is You, command me to come to You on the water." So He said, "Come." And when Peter had come down out of the boat, he walked on the water to go to Jesus. But when he saw that the wind was boisterous, he was afraid (Matthew 14:26,28-30).

Here's a question for you: Which is the greater marvel—the change in Peter that emboldened him to step out onto the water, or his brief walk on the water? Without question we would look at the physical act of walking on the water as a miracle from God, but something happened within Peter that was also a work of God. Here is a man who, being a fisherman, knew how treacherous the Sea of Galilee could be with its frequent strong winds. Perhaps he even knew of men who had drowned in it. Yet of all the frightened disciples, he alone stepped over the side of the boat to meet his Lord. He walked on water, but not far enough. The miracle went unfinished; Peter began to sink. As he watched the winds and the waves, fear overtook him and caused him to lose His focus—Jesus. Perhaps Peter looked back on that event the rest of his life, wondering why he allowed himself to be so distracted by the wind and the waves. Due to this distraction, the miracle that God was working both inside and outside Peter was interrupted. And how many of us are also unfinished miracles because we have become distracted by the challenges of life?

We know of a young man who, at 19, was a jobless high school dropout who busied himself by lying on the white, warm sands of a California beach and going to drinking parties with his pals. His parents, who prayed for him, were successful in getting him to go to church one evening. When the preacher ended his sermon with an invitation, to the astonishment of his mother, the young man rose and went forward. She was thrilled that her prayers had been answered and that God had begun to work a miracle in him.

The young man went to Bible college and preached in rescue missions, minimum-security prisons, and on the street corners of downtown San Diego. God's miracle in him was still developing. After Bible college, he went to graduate school and got a degree in Christian theology. Afterward he was offered the pastorate of a church with a good salary and a rent-free parsonage. But in the midst of all these blessings from God he became distracted by "the wind and the waves," and just like Peter, he began to lose the supernatural work of God in his life and sink. For the next 20 years or so, he pretty much lived apart from feeling any divine influence. He was an unfinished miracle.

Finally there came a time, very early one morning on a dark highway, when God unilaterally pulled this man back to Himself. The work of God was restarted in him. It continues to develop today even into the man's old age, but for the rest of his life he will regret having been distracted and wasting 20 years by not serving God as he should have. Understand that there was no miracle on his part—the miracle was God's alone.

The apostle Peter had also wandered out of the miraculous love, power, and grace of God when he grew fearful of the wind and the waves, and when he denied Jesus three times. But later, God graciously brought Peter back, and when some authorities threatened to jail him, he faced them with courage (Acts 4). And if tradition is correct, at the end of his life, Peter bravely joined his Lord by being crucified.

There is a divine work God wants to complete in each of us. Pray to God and offer yourself fully to Him. Pray with confidence in the knowledge that we do not come to Him by our worthiness, but by His lovingkindness.

The Pathways to Victory

God Has Not Given Us a Spirit of Fear

Fear is a natural reaction to suffering. Who among us would not be afraid to receive the news of cancer? Who would not be fearful to learn their child has a terminal disease? Who of us would not be terrified of the loss of a spouse or parent or close friend? With so much suffering in the world, we could easily resign ourselves to living in a constant state of fear. But this is not what God has called us to.

There was once a young pastor in a large city. Christianity had only recently come to this city, and the religious leaders who were already established there had begun to realize Christianity's threat to their way of life. The pastor was hounded constantly, and perhaps even feared for his life.

On top of external persecution, even within his own congregation, all was not well. Some people disparaged the pastor's youth. Others felt he was not adhering to tradition as much as he should. These grumblers were causing division in the church, and were in danger of walking away from their first love, Jesus Christ. The young pastor grieved over them to the point of weeping. His mentor and spiritual father heard of his affliction and sent letters of encouragement. He told the young pastor that he thanked God for his faith and service, and knew of his tears over the people. He then told the pastor, "God has not given us a spirit of fear, but of power and of love and of a sound mind" (2 Timothy 1:7).

The young pastor described above was Timothy, whom tradition tells us was the pastor of the church of Ephesus. It was the apostle Paul who encouraged Timothy by writing, "Do not be ashamed of the testimony of our Lord, nor of me His prisoner, but share with me in the sufferings for the gospel according to the power of God" (2 Timothy 1:8). Timothy's difficult circumstances were no reason to fear, and no reason to be ashamed of the gospel. We aren't entirely sure about how Timothy's life ended, but church tradition says he was martyred in A.D. 93 at the hands of pagans for his refusal to participate in an idolatrous ritual. If this is true, it seems Timothy heeded Paul's words and stood courageously in the face of danger.

In another letter, this one to the church in Rome, Paul reminded the Christians there that they had nothing to fear:

> You did not receive the spirit of bondage again to fear, but you received the Spirit of adoption by whom we cry out, "Abba, Father." The Spirit Himself bears witness with our spirit that we are children of God, and if children, then heirs—heirs of God and joint heirs with Christ, if indeed we suffer with Him, that we may also be glorified together (Romans 8:15-17).

What a wonderful assurance for us! As children of God through faith in Christ, we are heirs and we can cry to God, "Abba, Father." He can help us remain faithful in the face of suffering.

God Will Lift Us from Despair and Depression

In our modern era, depression is one of the most common diagnosed mental illnesses. An estimated 25 percent of Americans will experience depression at some point in their lives. Moreover, depression is one of the fastest-growing mental disorders, doubling since the 1980s. Three of the top seven prescribed drugs are antidepressants. Yet depression is often left untreated, leading to a life of suffering for the afflicted person, who doesn't know why he or she is depressed.

Christians are not immune from depression. Because a physical disorder is often the cause of depression, medication may be necessary, but Christians should not forget to seek the Lord's help to overcome whatever difficulties they may be experiencing. We have seen that God helps in times of need and suffering, and He can lift us from the enveloping darkness of despair and depression.

That was true about King David, who spent much time in despair when Saul was constantly threatening. After David became king, his own sons became his enemies, twice trying to take the kingdom from him. As we read through the book of Psalms, David's despair is vividly portrayed. Concerning his suffering at the hands of his enemies, David lamented, "LORD, how they have increased who trouble me! Many are they who rise up against me" (Psalm 3:1). Elsewhere he cried out, "I am weary with my groaning; all night I make my bed swim; I drench my couch with my tears. My eye wastes away because of grief; it grows old because of all my enemies" (Psalm 6:6-7).

David even believed God had forgotten him: "How long, O LORD? Will You forget me forever? How long will You hide Your face from me? How long shall I take counsel in my soul, having sorrow in my heart daily? How long will my enemy be exalted over me?" (Psalm 13:1-2).

However, David did not remain in depression. He cried out to the Lord for help: "You, O LORD, do not be far from Me; O My Strength, hasten to help Me!" (Psalm 22:19). And again, "Make haste to help me, O LORD, my salvation!" (38:22). The Lord answered David, coming to his aid: "I cried to the LORD with my voice, and He heard me from His holy hill" (Psalm 3:4). David said, "I sought the LORD, and He heard me, and delivered me from all my fears" (Psalm 34:4). For this David thanks the Lord: "I will extol You, O LORD, for You have lifted me up, and have not let my foes rejoice over me. O LORD my God, I cried out to You, and You healed me. O LORD, You brought my soul up from the grave; You have kept me alive, that I should not go down to the pit" (Psalm 30:1-3).

The first step in overcoming despair and depression is to cry out to the Lord. Medication may help the body, but only God can heal the spirit.

If anyone had reason to despair, it was the apostle Paul. Certainly we are all familiar with his trials and suffering. He recounts some of them in 1 Corinthians 11:24-29. He had been whipped five times, beaten with rods three times, stoned, shipwrecked three times, and threatened by robbers, his own people, the Gentiles, and false believers. He had been weary, hungry, thirsty, cold, and naked. And he said through all, he does not fall: "We are hard-pressed on every side, yet not crushed; we are perplexed, but not in despair; persecuted, but not forsaken; struck down, but not destroyed—always carrying about in the body the dying of the Lord Jesus, that the life of Jesus also may be manifested in our body" (2 Corinthians 4:8-10). At all times he was "carrying about" the gospel. It is what sustained him. Because of this he told the Corinthians,

> Therefore we do not lose heart. Even though our outward man is perishing, yet the inward man is being renewed day by day. For our light affliction, which is but for a moment, is working for us a far more exceeding and eternal weight of glory, while we do not look at the things which are seen, but at the things which are not seen. For the things which are seen are temporary, but the things which are not seen are eternal. For we know that if our earthly house, this tent, is destroyed, we have a building from God, a house not made with hands, eternal in the heavens. For in this we groan, earnestly desiring to be clothed with our habitation which is from heaven, if indeed, having been clothed, we shall not be found naked. For we who are in this tent groan, being burdened, not because we want to be unclothed, but further

clothed, that mortality may be swallowed up by life
(2 Corinthians 4:16–5:4).

Paul's groaning came not from the suffering he was enduring, but
from his desire to see the glory of heaven. Even if our suffering lasts
our entire life, in the end, God will lift us up to eternal glory. It is the
glorious finish to this earthly life for the believer that should encourage
us and help us through times of trouble.

God Will Not Give Us Difficulties We Cannot Bear

Not every trial is from God, but every trial is a chance to show our
faithfulness to God. In this way every difficulty is in a sense a trial,
and there is always a temptation to give in—just as Job's wife wrongly
advised Job to "curse God and die!" (Job 2:9). Indeed the whole book
of Job revolves around what path Job will follow. God allowed Job's
suffering for the purpose of testing his faith. Satan brought the suffering in an attempt to show that when things get tough, even the godly
crumble. While we are going through the suffering, our pain may
seem so great that we cannot bear it. The temptation to give up is very
strong. But we should not despair. Paul said, "God is faithful, who
will not allow you to be tempted beyond what you are able, but with
the temptation will also make the way of escape, that you may be able
to bear it" (1 Corinthians 10:13). No matter how dark the difficulty
seems, there is always a way out.

As humans, we may think there is no hope. We may deem the way
too difficult, or simply see things from the wrong perspective. This is
where meditation on the Scriptures is important. It is God's Word
that shows us the way through life's difficulties. Also, we should not
disregard wise and godly people around us. Sometimes all it takes to
make God's way of escape clear is an outside view. How many times
have we been given wise counsel that has helped us to see our situations more clearly?

James taught that we should have joy when we face trials, for "the
testing of your faith produces patience" (1:3). Through this patience,

we are made "perfect and complete" (verse 4). Part of this completeness is wisdom for dealing with trials. If we are lacking in this wisdom, we are to ask God for it in faith. James wrote, "Count it all joy when you fall into various trials, knowing that the testing of your faith produces patience" (James 1:2-3). This is not referring to salvation, for we know that salvation comes through faith in Christ. James is talking about the reward God gives for faithfulness.

In light of the hope we have in Christ, and the things we can gain from enduring, we must always keep Paul and James's encouragements in mind when we are enduring trials and temptations. God will never give us more than we can bear, and will always provide a way of escape. It is up to us to follow that way.

God Always Has a Way of Victory at the End

Count Earthly Things as Garbage—Even Suffering

In stark language, Paul portrayed this present, earthly life as nothing compared to Christ. In Philippians 3 he defended himself against those who argue that they are more righteous than Paul. They were taking confidence in the flesh—that is, activities they thought would gain them righteousness. Righteousness cannot be gained if suffering is self-imposed. Paul said that he, of all people, should know. Yet he said,

> What things were gain to me, these I have counted loss for Christ. Yet indeed I also count all things loss for the excellence of the knowledge of Christ Jesus my Lord, for whom I have suffered the loss of all things, and count them as rubbish, that I may gain Christ and be found in Him, not having my own righteousness, which is from the law, but that which is through faith in Christ, the righteousness which is from God by faith (Philippians 3:7-9).

The word "rubbish" in the New King James Version carries the idea of something completely lacking in any kind of value. The Greek word spoke of rotting flesh or animal excrement. The Jewish historian

Josephus used the term to describe what the besieged and starving residents of Jerusalem were finding to eat in the sewers. It is a vulgar term meant to catch people's attention. Paul said that anything we do of our own to gain righteousness with God is garbage, including self-caused suffering.

FORGETTING WHAT'S BEHIND AND PRESSING AHEAD

It is easy for us to be immobilized by our past. Perhaps we have endured such great suffering that it seems impossible to move beyond it. We are stuck in our thinking, seeing the present and future through the damaged lens of the past. If we are to lead a victorious life, however, which is the goal of all Christians, we must move forward.

Paul, after talking about how the things he had done in the past to gain righteousness were garbage, taught us to move beyond the past. He wrote, "One thing I do, forgetting those things which are behind and reaching forward to those things which are ahead, I press toward the goal for the prize of the upward call of God in Christ Jesus" (Philippians 3:13-14). No matter what suffering we may have endured in the past, we must always keep our eyes on the prize, our glorious reward in Christ.

STRIVING FOR A CROWN

Paul taught that the Christian life is like a race or a boxing match. He said,

> Do you not know that in a race all the runners compete, but only one receives the prize? So run that you may obtain it. Every athlete exercises self-control in all things. They do it to receive a perishable wreath, but we an imperishable. So I do not run aimlessly; I do not box as one beating the air. But I discipline my body and keep it under control, lest after preaching to others I myself should be disqualified (1 Corinthians 9:24-27 ESV).

We are to live our life with purpose, keeping in mind at all times the prize at the end of the race—the crown, the victory. We are not to live life wildly swinging at shadows, but in a disciplined manner so that we will avoid hypocrisy. This is how we avoid becoming derailed by suffering. And we are to avoid looking back, and always keep our focus forward.

Running coaches drill their running teams on the importance of never looking back, as doing so can cause a runner to lose focus and thereby lose precious seconds. Runners are taught to always think ahead about the next curve, the next hill, the next mile. Jesus taught the same principle: "No one, after putting his hand to the plow and looking back, is fit for the kingdom of God" (Luke 9:62 NASB).

This does not mean that someone who fails in the race or looks back will lose his salvation. Both Paul and Jesus were talking about discipleship—the act of living out our salvation, not gaining or losing it. The crown is not eternal life, but the eternal reward that God promises us. If we continually look back at our past suffering, we will miss out on the great prize, the crown, the everlasting reward of running the race victoriously.

The End of Suffering—Our Glorious Future

As Christians living through everyday life we may forget the glorious future we are promised in Scripture. The toils and troubles of this world constantly vie for our attention. And suffering can even cause us to lose focus, or fall into despair. We must remember that the sufferings of this world are not permanent. As we suffer, we should always keep in mind Paul's words of encouragement that we have nothing to fear in this life:

> Now this I say, brethren, that flesh and blood cannot inherit the kingdom of God; nor does corruption inherit incorruption. Behold, I tell you a mystery: We shall not all sleep, but we shall all be changed—in a moment, in the twinkling of an eye, at the last trumpet. For the trumpet will sound, and the dead will be raised incorruptible, and

we shall be changed. For this corruptible must put on incorruption, and this mortal must put on immortality. So when this corruptible has put on incorruption, and this mortal has put on immortality, then shall be brought to pass the saying that is written: "Death is swallowed up in victory."

"O Death, where is your sting? O Hades, where is your victory?" The sting of death is sin, and the strength of sin is the law. But thanks be to God, who gives us the victory through our Lord Jesus Christ.

Therefore, my beloved brethren, be steadfast, immovable, always abounding in the work of the Lord, knowing that your labor is not in vain in the Lord (1 Corinthians 15:50-58).

The corruption Paul spoke of is the fallen nature of things as they now stand. Everything, from our bodies to nature, has the taint of sin. Pain, disease, mental anguish, spiritual suffering, and all other forms of evil are the result of this corruption. This corruption also brings death. This book is a testament of the tremendous suffering taking place in our world. But this will not always be the case. Scripture tells us that one day, God will put an end to evil and suffering. This is what Paul is referring to—we should look forward to the fulfillment of this promise and let it drive us forward, as he said, "knowing that your labor is not in vain in the Lord."

Select Bibliography

"Does God feel our pain?" http://www.christiananswers.net/q-alia/god-pain.html (last accessed August 19, 2008).

"What kind of world would you create...if you were God?" http://www.christiananswers.net/gospe/gospel2.html (last accessed August 16, 2008).

Anselm. *Why God Became Man.*

Aquinas, St. Thomas. *Summa Theologica*

Arndt, William F. and F. Wilber Gingrich. *A Greek–English Lexicon of the New Testament.* Chicago: University Press, 1957.

Athanasius. *Incarnation of the Word.*

Augustine. *On the Trinity.*

Bauckham, Richard. "'Only the Suffering God Can help' divine passibility in modern theology." *Themelios,* April 1984, 6-12. http://www.theologicalstudies.org.uk/article_god_bauckham.html (last accessed August 15, 2008).

Bray, Gerald. "Can God Suffer?" http://www.theologian.org.uk/doctrine/cangodssuffer.html (last accessed August 15, 2008).

Brown, F., S.R. Driver, and C.A. Briggs, *A Hebrew and English Lexicon of the Old Testament.* Oxford: Clarendon Press, 1907.

Calvin, John. *Institutes of the Christian Religion,* trans. Henry Beveridge. Grand Rapids: Eerdmans, 1979.

Chemnitz, Martin. *The Two Natures in Christ.* Saint Louis: Concordia, 1971.

Erickson, Millard J. *Christian Theology.* Grand Rapids: Baker, 1989.

Gavrilyuk, Paul. *The Suffering of the Impassible God: The Dialectics of Patristic Thought.* Oxford: Oxford University Press, 2006.

Geisler, Norman L. and H. Wayne House, *The Battle for God*. Grand Rapids: Kregel, 2001.

Geisler, Norman. *Systematic Theology*, vol. II. Minneapolis: Bethany, 2003.

Grudem, Wayne. *Systematic Theology*. Grand Rapids: Zondervan, 1994.

Helm, Paul. Divine Impassibility: Why Is It Suffering? Reformation21. http://www.reformation21.org/Past_Issues/2006_Issues_1_16_Articles/Divine_Impassibility/94 (last accessed August 20, 2008).

Hodge, Charles. *Systematic Theology*. Grand Rapids: Eerdmans, 1981.

House, H. Wayne, "Does the Doctrine of the Impassibility of God Invalidate Orthodox Theism?" (unpublished paper).

House, H. Wayne. "God, Gender and Biblical Metaphor" in *Journal of Biblical Manhood and Womanhood*. Spring 2005, 63-71.

Johnson, Phillip R. "God Without Mood Swings: Recovering the Doctrine of Divine Impassibility." http://www.spurgeon.org/~phil/articles/impassib.htm (last accessed August 15, 2008).

Kempf, Constantin. "Theodicy" *Catholic Encyclopedia*. http://www.newadvent.org/cathen/14569a.htm (last accessed August 20, 2008).

Leibniz, Gottfried Wilhelm. "Theodicy: Abridgement of the Argument Reduced to Syllogistic Form." http://www.class.uidaho.edu/mickelsen/texts/Leibniz%20-%20Theodicy.htm (last accessed August 16, 2008).

McAllister, Dawson. "If God knows I am hurting, why doesn't He help me?" http://images.google.com/imgres?imgurl=http://www.christiananswers.net (last accessed August 20, 2008).

Murray, Michael. "Leibniz on the Problem of Evil" in *Stanford Encyclopedia of Philosophy*, http://plano.stanford.edu/entries/leibniz-evil (last accessed August 15, 2008).

Nelson, Haydn D. *The Providence of God: A Trinitarian Perspective*. Unpublished thesis for Doctor of Philosophy, Murdoch University, 2005.

Passantino, Bob and Gretchen. "If God Is Good, Why Is There So Much Suffering in the World?" http://www.answers.org/theology/suffering.html (last accessed August 15, 2008).

Pieper, Francis. *Christian Dogmatics*, vol. II. St. Louis: Concordia, 1951, 157-68.

Shedd, William G.T. *Dogmatic Theology*. Nashville: Nelson, 1980.

Strong, A.H. *Systematic Theology*. Valley Forge: Judson, 1907.

Strong, Augustus. *Systematic Theology*. Valley Forge: Judson, 1967.

Warfield, Benjamin Breckinridge. *The Person and Work of Christ*. Philadelphia: Presbyterian & Reformed, 1070.

Weinandy, Thomas G. "Does God Suffer?" Le Penseur Réfléchit, http://www .mrrena.com/2004/suffer.shtml (last accessed August 15, 2008).

Weinandy, Thomas G. *Does God Suffer?* Notre Dame, IN: University of Notre Dame Press, 2000.

Zacharias, Ravi. "I Feel Your Pain." http://www.rzim.org/GlobalElements/GFV /tabid/449/ArticleID/9282/CBModuleID/1133/Default.aspx (last accessed August 16, 2008).

Notes

Chapter 1—God and Human Suffering

1. For further discussion of heretical "Christian" groups, see H. Wayne House, *Charts of Cults, Sects, and Religious Movements* (Grand Rapids: Zondervan, 2000); H. Wayne House and Gordon Carle, *Doctrine Twisting: How Core Biblical Doctrines are Distorted* (Downers Grove, IL: InterVarsity Press, 2003); and H. Wayne House, *Charts of World Religions* (Grand Rapids: Zondervan, 2006).

2. *Trust and Obey* by John H. Sammis, 1887.

3. Richard Dawkins, *The God Delusion* (New York: Houghton Mifflin, 2006), 31, 38, 248.

4. Richard Dawkins, "Ignorance Is No Crime," *Free Inquiry Magazine*, Vol. 21, No. 3, 2001.

5. "Does Jesus Care?" by Frank E. Graeff, 1901.

6. Daryl Witmer, "Does God feel our pain?" http://www.christian answers.net/q-alia/god-pain.html (last accessed August 21, 2008).

7. "Study: Many Americans Believe God More Powerful at Saving Lives Than Doctors," Monday, August 18, 2008 http://www.foxnews .com/story/0,2933,405765,00.html. The physicians in this case were encouraged to console them and maneuver them to rely on medical treatment.

8. Zacharias, Ravi. "I Feel Your Pain," http://www.rzim.org/Global Elements/GFV/tabid/449/ArticleID/9282/CBModuleID/1133 /Default.aspx (last accessed August 16, 2008).

Chapter 2—Why All the Misery in the World?

1. Matthew Henry, *Matthew Henry's Commentary on the Whole Bible* (Peabody, MA: Hendrickson, 1996), Genesis 2:21.

2. Quoted in Tom Davis, et al., "A Failure of Initiative: The Final Report of the Select Bipartisan Committee to Investigate the Preparation for and Response to Hurricane Katrina," http://katrina.house.gov/full_katrina_report.htm 111-112 (last accessed August 23, 2008).

3. Raymond Seed, et al., "Preliminary Report on the Performance of the New Orleans Levee Systems in Hurricane Katrina on August 29, 2005," Center for Information Technology Research in the Interest of Society (University of California Berkeley), November 2, 2005. Quoted from "Katrina: What Happened When," Annenberg Public Policy Center of the University of Pennsylvania, http://www.factcheck.org/article348.html (last accessed August 23, 2008).

4. Drew Griffin and Kyra Phillips, "Witnesses: New Orleans cops among looters," CNN, Friday, September 30, 2005, http://www.cnn.com/2005/US/09/29/nopd.looting/index.html (last accessed on August 23, 2008).

5. Theodore Dalrymple, *Life at the Bottom* (Chicago: Ivan R. Dee, 2001), 36.

6. Dalrymple, *Life,* 137.

Chapter 3—Why Has God Allowed Evil in the World?

1. Al-Ghazali, quoted in Eleanore Stump and Michael J. Murray, eds., *Philosophy of Religion* (Malden, MA: Blackwell, 1990), 191.

2. Norman Geisler, *Philosophy of Religion* (Grand Rapids: Zondervan, 1974), 313.

3. See Norman Geisler and H. Wayne House, *The Battle for God* (Grand Rapids: Kregel), 2001.

4. Harold S. Kushner, "When Bad Things Happen to Good People," excerpt as an article from *When Bad Things Happen to Good People,* http://www.myjewishlearning.com/ideas_belief/sufferingevil/Suffering_Solutions_TO/Suffering_Modern_Responses/Suffering_When_Kushner.htm (last accessed August 26, 2008).

5. Ibid.

6. Ibid.

7. Ibid.

8. Ibid.

9. Ibid.

10. Geisler, *Philosophy,* 336.

11. Geisler, *Philosophy,* 339.

12. James R. Boyd, ed., *The Westminster Shorter Catechism* (New York: M.W. Dodd, 1856), 19.

13. This does not mean, as some have argued, that we were created without the ability to be influenced, or have our freedom hindered. When

Adam introduced sin into the world, our nature was corrupted, and with it the free exercise of our will. The Scriptures are clear that this corruption was passed on to all of Adam's descendants. Unless God repairs our corrupted will, we will always be hindered in our freedom.

14. One needs to understand that the move to establish a nation in the ancient Jewish homeland actually began in the nineteenth century with the work of Theodor Herzl, who started the original Zionist movement.

Chapter 4—Why Does God Allow Pain in Our Lives?

1. I (Wayne) sang this song back in the early 1960s, and it was an old song even then, but I have been unable to locate the original source.

2. For the story of Corrie ten Boom, read *The Hiding Place* (Old Tappan, NJ: Revell, 1976), which was made into a movie.

3. Paul Jacobs and Hartmut Krienke, "Proginosko" in *The New International Dictionary of New Testament Theology*, vol. 1, ed. Colin Brown (Grand Rapids: Regency, 1967), 693.

4. Douglas Moo, *The Epistle to the Romans,* The New International Commentary on the New Testament, ed. Gordon D. Fee (Grand Rapids: Eerdmans, 1966), 674.

5. Gregory A. Boyd, "The Open Theism View" in *Divine Foreknowledge, Four Views,* eds. James K. Beilby and Paul R. Eddy (Downer's Grove, IL: InterVarsity, 2001), 14. Boyd asserts that God did not "settle" all that will happen. See the refutation of the Open Theism heresy in Norman L. Geisler and H. Wayne House, with Max Herrera, in *The Battle for God* (Grand Rapids: Kregel, 2000).

6. "Why We Must Preach Prosperity," found at http://www.believers.org/believe/bel102.htm (last accessed December 11, 2007).

7. See Theodore Dalrymple, *Life at the Bottom: The Worldview that Makes the Underclass* (Chicago: Ivan R. Dee, 2003); and Our Culture, What's Left of It: The Mandarins and the Masses (Chicago: Ivan R. Dee, 2005).

8. Murray J. Harris, "Second Corinthians" in *The Expositor's Bible Commentary,* vol. 10, ed. Frank E. Gaebelein (Grand Rapids: Zondervan, 1977), 396. Philip Edgcumbe Hughes, "Paul's Second Epistle to the Corinthians" in *The New International Commentary on The New Testament,* ed. F.F. Bruce (Grand Rapids: Eerdmans,1962), 442-48.

9. Roland Bainton, *Here I Stand, a Life of Martin Luther* (New York: Abingdon, 1950), 41-67.

10. Philip Schaff, *History of the Christian Church,* vol. 2 (Grand Rapids: Eerdmans,1979), 66.

11. *Fox's Book of Martyrs,* ed. William Byron Forbush (Chicago: Winston, 1926), 29.

12. Gregory of Nyssa, *Against Eunomius,* Book V, 3 (*NPNF*² 5:176).

13. While *peirasmos* may mean either trial or temptation, in Hebrews 4:15 it must include being tempted, as the text says that Christ has been tempted as we are.

Chapter 5—Getting to Know the God Who Cares for You

1. A.W. Tozer, *The Knowledge of the Holy* (New York: Harper & Row, 1961), 10.

2. Tozer, *The Knowledge of the Holy,* 9.

3. St. Augustine, *Confessions,* Book 1, 1.1.1, quoted from Augustine's *Confessions,* translated by E.B. Pusey, http://ccat.sas.upenn.edu/jod /augustine/Pusey/book01 (last accessed August 29, 2008): "tu excitas, ut laudare te delectet, quia fecisti nos ad te et inquietem est cor nostrum, donec requiescat in te." Latin from *Augustini Confessiones,* http://ccat.sas.upenn.edu/jod/latinconf/latinconf.html (last accessed August 29, 2008).

4. Brian Davies, *The Reality of God and the Problem of Evil* (United Kingdom: Continuum, 2006), 78.

5. C.J. Labuschagne, *The Incomparability of Yahweh in the Old Testament* (Leiden, Netherlands: E.J. Brill, 1966).

6. Labuschagne, *The Incomparability of Yahweh in the Old Testament,* 8-15.

7. Also see Deuteronomy 33:26; 2 Samuel 7:22; 1 Kings 8:23; 1 Chronicles 17:20.

8. Labuschagne, *The Incomparability of Yahweh in the Old Testament,* 16-23.

9. Also see Deuteronomy 3:24; 4:7; Job 36:22; Psalm 35:10; 77:14; 89:9.

10. Labuschagne, *The Incomparability of Yahweh in the Old Testament,* 28-30.

11. For further argument on the New Testament's presentation of God's uniqueness, see Jerome H. Neyrey, *Give God the Glory: Ancient Prayer and Worship in Cultural Perspective* (Grand Rapids: Eerdmans, 2007), 125-43.

12. The text of Theophilus is from Maroslav Markovich, *Theophilil Antiocheni ad Autolycum* (Berlin: De Gruyter, 1995), 18; quoted from Jerome H. Neyrey, *Give God the Glory: Ancient Prayer and Worship in Cultural Perspective* (Grand Rapids: Eerdmans, 2007), 130. I have removed the Greek words from the quotation (emphasizing by italics the English words that stand for the Greek words) and included them with the text in this footnote for one who desires to examine the terminology: "The appearance of God is ineffable (*arreton*) and indescribable (*anekphraston*) and cannot be seen by eyes of flesh. In

glory God is incomprehensible (*achoregos*), in greatness unfathomable (*akataleptos*), in height inconceivable (*aperinontos*), in power incomparable (*asugkritos*), in wisdom unrivaled (*asumbibastos*), in goodness inimitable (*amimetos*), in kindness unutterable (*anekdiegetos*).

13. This text is from *Kerygma tou Petrou*, found in Michael Cambre, *Kerygma Petri Textus et Commenatrius* (Turnhout: Brepols, 2003), 151; quoted from Jerome H. Neyrey, *Give God the Glory: Ancient Prayer and Worship in Cultural Perspective* (Grand Rapids: Eerdmans, 2007), 143. I have removed the Greek words from the quotation (emphasizing by italics the English words that stand for the Greek words) and included them with the text in this footnote for one who desires to examine the terminology:

> Recognize now that there is one God
>
> …the Invisible (*aoratos*) who sees (*hora*) all things;
>
> the Incomprehensible (*achoretos*) who comprehends (*chorei*) all things;
>
> the One who needs nothing (*anepidees*), of whom all things stand in need (*epideitai*),
>
> the Uncreated (*apoietos*), who made (*epoiesen*) all things by the word of His power.

14. Nicholas of Cusa, *The Vision of God* (New York: E.P. Dutton & Sons, 1928), 60; quoted in A.W. Tozer, *The Knowledge of the Holy* (New York: Harper & Row, 1961), 16.

15. Nicholas of Cusa, *The Vision of God,* 58-59; quoted in A.W. Tozer, *The Knowledge of the Holy* (New York: Harper & Row, 1961), 16.

16. Tozer, *The Knowledge of the Holy,* 14.

17. ánaḥ: *Theological Wordbook of the Old Testament,* R. Laird Harris, ed. (Chicago: Moody, 1980), electronic text used by permission. Version 1.4. Also see jn"a; F. Brown, S.R. Driver, and C.A. Briggs. *A Hebrew and English Lexicon of the Old Testament* (abridged), *A Hebrew and English Lexicon of the Old Testament* (Oxford: Clarendon Press, 1907). Digitized and abridged as a part of the Princeton Theological Seminary Hebrew Lexicon Project under the direction of Dr. J.M. Roberts. Used by permission. Electronic text corrected, formatted, and hypertexted by OakTree Software, Inc. This electronic adaptation © 2001 OakTree Software, Inc., Version 3.2.

18. zaʻaq: *Theological Wordbook of the Old Testament.*

19. šawʻah: *Theological Wordbook of the Old Testament.*

20. ne'aqah: *A Hebrew and English Lexicon of the Old Testament.*

21. šamaʻ: *A Hebrew and English Lexicon of the Old Testament.*

22. zakar: *A Hebrew and English Lexicon of the Old Testament.*

23. ra'a: *A Hebrew and English Lexicon of the Old Testament.*

24. W. MacDonald and A. Farstad, *Believer's Bible Commentary: Old and New Testaments* (Nashville: Thomas Nelson, 1997), Exodus 2:23.

25. yada: *Theological Lexicon of the Old Testament,* Ernst Jenni, ed. (Peabody, MA: Hendrickson Publishers, 1997). Used by permission. Electronic text hypertexted and prepared by OakTree Software, Inc. Version 2.0

Chapter 6—Can God Experience Pain?

1. William Hendriksen, *The Gospel of John,* New Testament Commentary (Grand Rapids: Baker, 1976), 167 (emphasis mine).

2. A.H. Strong, *Systematic Theology* (Valley Forge, PA: Judson, 1907), 1.

3. Millard J. Erickson, *Christian Theology* (Grand Rapids: Baker, 1989), 265.

4. Charles Hodge, *Systematic Theology,* vol. 1, (Grand Rapids: Eerdmans, 1986), 369; Robert L. Reymond, *A New Systematic Theology of the Christian Faith* (Nashville: Nelson, 1998), 161.

5. Strong, *Systematic Theology,* 245.

6. William G.T. Shedd, *Dogmatic Theology,* vol. 1 (Nashville: Nelson, 1980), 335; H. Orton Wiley, *Christian Theology,* vol. 1 (Kansas City: Beacon Hill, 1940), 321.

7. Shedd, *Theology,* 351.

8. Hodge, *Theology,* 390.

9. Hodge, *Theology,* 391.

10. Aquinas, *Suma,* 101.

11. E.W. Bullinger, *Figures of Speech Used in the Bible* (Grand Rapids: Baker, 1968), 871.

12. Norman L. Geisler and H. Wayne House, *The Battle for God* (Grand Rapids: Kregel, 2001), 92.

13. J.B. Lightfoot, *Saint Paul's Epistles to the Colossians and to Philemon* (Grand Rapids: Zondervan, 1969), 182.

14. David W. Diehl, "Process Theology" in *Evangelical Dictionary of Theology,* Walter A. Elwell, ed. (Grand Rapids: Baker, 1989), 880.

15. Betty J. Eadie, *Embraced by the Light* (Placerville, CA: Gold Leaf Press, 1992), 45.

16. Ibid., 47.

17. Ibid., 81.

18. Shirley MacLaine, *Out on a Limb* (New York: Bantam, 1986), 181, 234, 235.

19. Ibid., 317.

20. Ibid., 209.

21. Ibid., 326.

22. James Van Praagh, *Talking to Heaven* (New York: Signet, 1999), 270.

23. Ibid. 291.

24. Shedd, *Theology,* vol. 2, 387.

25. Norman Geisler, *Systematic Theology,* vol. 2 (Minneapolis: Bethany, 2003), 112.

26. For example, Wayne Grudem, *Systematic Theology* (Grand Rapids: Zondervan, 1994), 165.

27. Wayne Grudem, *Systematic Theology* (Grand Rapids: Zondervan, 1994), 166.

28. Clark H. Pinnock, *The Openness of God* (Downer's Grove, IL: Inter-Varsity, 1994), 46.

29. John B. Cobb Jr. and David Ray Griffin, *Process Theology* (Philadelphia: Westminster, 1976) 52, 42.

30. Lewis Sperry Chafer, *Systematic Theology,* vol. 1 (Dallas: Dallas Seminary Press, 1974), 228.

31. Strong, *Theology,* 353.

Chapter 7—Did God Suffer When Christ Died on the Cross?

1. Millard J. Erickson, *God in Three Persons* (Grand Rapids: Baker, 1984), 223.

2. Millard J. Erickson. *Christian Theology* (Grand Rapids: Baker, 1983), 710.

3. Ibid., 735.

4. John Calvin, *Institutes of the Christian Religion,* II:XIII:4 (emphases added).

5. The following is only a small representation of the perspectives of orthodox church fathers and theologians of the church:

   > Tertullian: Now, although two substances are alleged to be in Christ-namely, the divine and the human...it plainly follows that the divine nature is immortal, and that the human is mortal... that which died was the nature which was anointed; in a word, the flesh...for we do not maintain that he died after the divine nature, but only after the human...You have Him exclaiming in the midst of His passion: My God, My God, why hast Thou forsaken Me?...But this was the voice of flesh and soul, that is to say, of man...that is to say, not of God; and, it was uttered to show the impassibility of God, who forsook His Son, so far as He handed

over His human substance to the suffering of death (Tertullian, *Against Praxeas,* 29).

John of Damascus: He has corresponding to the two natures, the Two sets of natural qualities (i.e., qualities of the natures); two natural volitions, one divine and one human, two natural energies, one divine and one human, two natural free-wills, one divine and one human, two kinds of wisdom and knowledge, one divine and one human…we hold that wills and energies are faculties belonging to nature not to subsistence (John of Damascus, *Exposition of the Orthodox Faith,* III:XIII, XIV).

Anselm: For we affirm that the divine nature is undoubtedly incapable of suffering, and cannot in any sense be brought low from its exalted standing, and cannot labour with difficulty over what it wishes to do. But we say that the Lord Jesus is true God and true man, one Person in two nature and two natures in one Person. In view of this, when we say that God is suffering some humiliation or weakness, we do not understand this in terms of the exaltedness of his non-suffering nature, but in terms of the weakness of the human substance which he was taking upon himself (Anselm, *Why God Became Man,* 1:8).

Chemnitz, the Lutheran reformer: Thus it follows of necessity that as the person of Christ has two complete and distinct natures, so also as the Damascenus (the one cited above)…says, "He has double or two-fold qualities which correspond to these two natures. He assumed a nature which was intelligent, possessed of a will, operative or effective. Thus with the human nature He also assumed the power of understanding, willing, and working qualities which are proper to and arranged for human nature…those who deny that the incarnate Christ possesses human knowledge, will, and activity, at the same time also deny the reality of His essence or of his human nature…each nature performs in communion with the other that which is proper to it. (Martin Chemnitz, *The Two Natures in Christ* [Saint Louis: Concordia, 1971] 235, 237).

6. Augustine, *On the Trinity,* Book V, Chapter 2.

7. William Ellery Channing, *Unitarian Christianity in Readings in the History of Christian Thought,* ed. Robert L. Ferm (New York: Holt, Rinehart, & Winston, 1964), 100.

8. Augustine. *On the Trinity,* Book I, Chapter 7.

9. Gregory of Nyssa. *Against Apollinarius,* http://www.sage.edu/faculty /salomd/nyssa/appolin.html (last accessed August 17, 2008).

Chapter 8—How Do We Participate in Christ's Sufferings?

1. Interpretations 1–4 are discussed in Peter T. O'Brien, *Colossians and Philemon,* Word Biblical Commentary (Waco: Word Books, 1982), 77-78.

2. As discussed in Heinrich August Wilhem Meyer, *Critical and Exegetical Handbook to the Epistles to the Philippians and Colossians and to Philemon* (New York: Funk & Wagnall, 1885), 255.

3. This is the opinion of Richard R. Melick, Jr. *Philippians, Colossians, Philemon,* The New American Commentary (Nashville, TN: Broadman, 1991), 239. Also see James D.G. Dunn, *The Epistles to Colossians and Philemon,* in New International Greek Testament Commentary (Grand Rapids: Eerdmans, 1996), 115-16.

4. Curtis Vaughn, "Colossians," *Expositor's Bible Commentary,* Frank E. Gaebelein, ed. (Grand Rapids: Zondervan, 1978), 190.

5. Ronald F. Youngblood, ed., *Nelson's New Illustrated Bible Dictionary,* (Nashville: Nelson, 1995), 954.

6. R. Schippers, "Fullness," *The New International Dictionary of New Testament Theology,* vol. 1, Colin Brown, ed. (Grand Rapids: Regency, 1967), 741.

7. Murray J. Harris, *The Second Epistle to the Corinthians* (Grand Rapids: Eerdmans, 2005), 149.

8. Norval Geldenhuys. *Commentary on the Gospel of Luke,* The New International Commentary on the New Testament, N.B. Stonehouse, ed. (Grand Rapids: Eerdmans, 1951), 276.

9. Douglas J. Moo. *The Epistle to the Romans,* The New International Commentary on the New Testament, Gordon D. Fee, ed. (Grand Rapids: Eerdmans, 1996), 505.

Chapter 10—Being Victorious in the Face of Life's Problems

1. This is currently the preferred term to use for what was formerly called *mental retardation,* which itself was a medically acceptable substitution for numerous pejorative terms. "Mental Retardation," http://en.wikipedia.org/wiki/Mental_retardation (last accessed September 5, 2008).

2. John Newton, *Amazing Grace,* http://en.wikipedia.org/wiki/Amazing_Grace (last accessed September 5, 2008).

3. Walter L. Liefeld, "Luke," *Expositor's Bible Commentary,* Frank E. Gaebelein, ed. (Grand Rapids: Zondervan, 1984), 904.

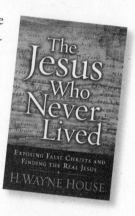